Company's Coming®

Potato
Favourites

Paré • Pirk • Darcy

Distributed by
Canada Book Distributors
11414-119 Street
Edmonton. Alberta, Canada T5G 2X6
Tel: 1-800-661-9017

Library and Archives Canada Cataloguing in Publication

Paré, Jean, 1927–, author
        Potato favourites / Paré, Pirk, Darcy.

Includes index.
Issued in print and electronic formats.
ISBN 978-1-77207-053-8 (softcover).–ISBN 978-1-77207-054-5 (EPUB)
        1. Cooking (Potatoes). 2 . Cookbooks. I. Pirk, Wendy,
1973–, author II. Darcy, James, 1956–, author III. Title.
IV. Title: At head of title: Company's Coming.

TX803.P8P365 2019   641.6'521   C2018-905689-4
                                                                 C2018-906571-0

Front Cover: ALLEKO; Background: Tatiana Volgutova; Front flap, top: Bartosz Luczak

All inside photos by Company's coming except: from gettyimages: Aleksandr_Vorobev, 17; alexbai, 63; ALLEKO, 99; AmalliaEka, 107; Azurita, 119; bhofack2, 1, 39, 123; Cglade, 7b; Christian-Fischer, 41; Diana Taliun, 7d; DreamBigPhotos, 129; elena_hramowa, 135; ElenaTaurus, 125; emiu, 29; etorres69, 87; EzumeImages, 49; Fred Chaveton, 16; from_my_ point_of_view, 77; grafvision, 15; iko636, 133; IngridHS, 97; Irina_Meliukh, 157; istetianae, 27; izhairguns, 71; jmillard37, 62; joannawnuk, 143; katerinabelaya, 147; Lilechka75, 93; Lisovskaya, 6; lucop, 145; margouillatphotos, 5, 33; Mariha-kitchen, 53, 57, 83; molka, 31; nata_vkusidey, 67; NatashaBreen, 160; Nebari, 7c; NoirChocolate, 51; OksanaKiian, 61, 75, 89, 121; paulfourk, 21; philipimage, 139; piolka, 23; Piotr Krzeslak, 85, 115; Rimma_ Bondarenko, 105; Smartstock, 7a; solomonjee, 9; Tatiana Volgutova, 79; tycoon751, 103; vaaseenaa, 149; VeselovaElena, 19; yasuhiroamano, 95; YelenaYemchuk, 127.

We acknowledge the financial support of the Government of Canada.
Nous reconnaissons l'appui financier du gouvernement du Canada.

Funded by the Government of Canada | Canadä
Financé par le gouvernement du Canada

PC: 38

Table of Contents

The Jean Paré Story

Jean Paré (pronounced "jeen PAIR-ee") grew up understanding that the combination of family, friends and home cooking is the best recipe for a good life. When Jean left home, she took with her a love of cooking, many family recipes and an intriguing desire to read cookbooks as if they were novels!

"Never share a recipe you wouldn't use yourself."

When her four children had all reached school age, Jean volunteered to cater the 50th anniversary celebration of the Vermilion School of Agriculture, now Lakeland College, in Alberta, Canada. Working from her home, Jean prepared a dinner for more than 1,000 people and from there launched a flourishing catering operation that continued for more than 18 years.

As requests for her recipes increased, Jean was often asked, "Why don't you write a cookbook?" The release of *150 Delicious Squares* on April 14, 1981, marked the debut of what would soon turn into one of the world's most popular cookbook series.

Company's Coming cookbooks are distributed in Canada, the United States, Australia and other world markets. Bestsellers many times over in English, Company's Coming cookbooks have also been published in French and Spanish.

Familiar and trusted in home kitchens around the world, Company's Coming cookbooks are offered in a variety of formats. Highly regarded as kitchen workbooks, the softcover Original Series, with its lay-flat plastic comb binding, is still a favourite among home cooks.

Jean Paré's approach to cooking has always called for quick and easy recipes using everyday ingredients. That view served her well, and the tradition continues in the Practical Gourmet series.

Jean's Golden Rule of Cooking is: Never share a recipe you wouldn't use yourself. It's an approach that has worked—millions of times over!

Introduction

You would have to look long and hard to find a vegetable that is more versatile than the potato. This humble tuber has a place at every meal, from breakfast to dessert. It can act as a side, complementing the main course, or it can step into the limelight and serve as the main attraction. Inexpensive, nutritious and delicious, the modest spud can't be beat for its role in economical, diverse dishes the whole family will love.

To get the most from your potatoes, keep these simple guidelines in mind:

Buying Tips

- Choose potatoes that are firm and heavy for their size.

- Avoid those that have green or black spots, bruises or sprouts. Green spots on the skin indicate the potato was exposed to sunlight as it was growing or during storage and may contain an alkaloid called solanine. Solanine has a bitter flavour and can be toxic if eaten in large quantities. Potatoes that have sprouted are still edible but will have lost much of their nutritional value.

- Unless you have a cold room to keep them in, buy only as many potatoes as you will use within a week or two.

Proper Storage

- To keep your potatoes fresh as long as possible, store them in a cool, dark place, in an open container or bowl with good ventilation so they can breathe. Do not keep them in a plastic bag, or you will shorten their shelf life.

- Never store raw potatoes in the fridge because the starches will convert to sugar, giving the potatoes an unpleasant sweet flavour.

- Store potatoes away from onions because both potatoes and onions release natural gasses that can cause each other to rot.

- Potatoes can be stored for months in a cold room but are best used within a few days if stored in a dark cupboard. If you notice one potato starting to soften or rot, remove it immediately as it will cause all those around it to do the same.

- You can freeze cooked mashed potatoes and stuffed potatoes, but do not freeze raw potatoes; they become soft and unappetizing.

To Peel or Not to Peel

Whether or not to peel your potatoes is really a matter of preference. Much of the potato's fibre and nutrients are in the skin, so peeling results in a loss of nutritional value. For most recipes, scrub the potatoes clean before cooking them. However, some dishes just taste better without the skin, so if you must peel your potatoes, do so after they have been cooked and take only a thin layer to minimize the amount of flavour and nutrients lost.

All Potatoes are NOT Created Equal

The key to success when cooking with potatoes is to choose the right potato for the job. With more than 4000 varieties of potatoes available, you can be sure that some types perform in certan dishes better than others. Thankfully, potatoes can be grouped into 3 general categories, which can help you choose which potato will work best in the dish you want to prepare.

Baking

Types: includes Baker, Russet (you can tell if a potato is starchy by the white film left on your knife when you cut it)

Best uses: baking, frying, mashing; okay in a blended cream soup but not if you want potato chunks; do not use in potato salads

Characteristics: thick, rough skin; usually oblong shaped; higher starch content; does not hold its shape when cooked

Waxy

Types: includes fingerlings and most new and red potatoes

Best uses: boiling, roasting; great in soups; not suitable for baked or mashed potatoes

Characteristics: thin, papery skin that rubs off when you scratch it with your fingernail; firm, creamy texture; lower starch content; keeps its shape when cooked.

All-purpose

Types: includes Yukon Gold, Bintje

Best uses: baking, frying, boiling, roasting, mashing; truly an all-purpose potato

Characteristics: usually white to yellow flesh; red or yellowish skin; oblong or round shape; is between baking and waxy for starch content

Sweet Potatoes

Types: Jewel, Garnet, Hannah

Best uses: often interchangeable with regular potatoes; mash, bake, roast

Characteristics: white to orange skin and flesh; usually oblong and irregularly shaped; texture ranges from dry to wet; sweet flavour

Samosas

Potatoes in a potato crust with exotic East Indian flavours. These samosas take a little longer to prepare, but the final result is well worth it. If you prefer to deep-fry your samosas, cook a few at a time in 375°F (190°C) cooking oil for 3 1/2 to 4 minutes until golden brown (there is no need to brush them with egg first). Remove with a slotted spoon to paper towels to drain.

Mashed baking potatoes (see Note)	2 cups	500 mL
Large egg, fork-beaten	1	1
All-purpose flour	1 1/4 cups	300 mL
Salt	1/2 tsp.	2 mL
Diced cooked potato	1 1/2 cups	375 mL
Frozen peas, thawed	1/2 cup	125 mL
Ground cumin	3/4 tsp.	4 mL
Cayenne pepper	1/4 tsp.	1 mL
Turmeric	1/4 tsp.	1 mL
Ground coriander	1/2 tsp.	2 mL
Salt	1/2 tsp.	2 mL
Large egg, fork-beaten	1	1

For the crust, combine first 4 ingredients in a medium bowl to form a soft ball of dough. Roll 1/2 of dough out on a well-floured surface in 11 x 14 inch (28 x 35 cm) rectangle. Cut into 3 1/2 inch (9 cm) squares.

For the filling, combine next 7 ingredients in a medium bowl. Spoon 1 tbsp. (15 mL) onto one side of centre in each square. Dampen two adjoining sides. Fold over diagonally and seal edges.

Brush tops with egg. Place on a greased baking sheet. Bake in 400°F (200°C) oven for 14 to 15 minutes. Repeat with remaining dough and filling. Makes 24 samosas.

1 samosa: 50 Calories; 0.5 g Total Fat (0 g Mono, 0 g Poly, 0 g Sat); 20 mg Cholesterol; 10 g Carbohydrate (1 g Fibre, trace Sugar); 2 g Protein; 105 mg Sodium

Note: Baking potatoes are best for the crust because of their dry texture. They can be used for the filling as well.

Potato Salad Bites

Creamy potato salad is transformed into a neat handheld starter with these appealing bites.

Spreadable cream cheese	1/2 cup	125 mL
Finely chopped red pepper	2 tbsp.	30 mL
Grated medium Cheddar cheese	2 tbsp.	30 mL
Grated Parmesan cheese	2 tbsp.	30 mL
Mayonnaise	2 tbsp.	30 mL
Thinly sliced green onion	2 tbsp.	30 mL
Garlic powder	1/4 tsp.	1 mL
Paprika	1/8 tsp.	0.5 mL
Pepper	1/8 tsp.	0.5 mL
Baby potatoes, halved (about 1 1/2 lbs., 680 g)	20	20
Salt	1 tsp.	5 mL

Fresh parsley leaves, for garnish

Combine first 9 ingredients in a small bowl. Chill.

Pour water into a large saucepan until about 1 inch (2.5 cm) deep. Add potatoes and salt. Bring to a boil. Reduce heat to medium and boil gently, covered, for 12 to 15 minutes until tender. Drain. Rinse with cold water and drain well. Trim bottom of each potato half to make it flat. Arrange potatoes, trimmed-side down, on a platter. Spoon about 1 tsp. (5 mL) cream cheese mixture onto each potato half.

Garnish with parsley leaves. Makes 40 bites.

1 bite: 30 Calories; 1.5 g Total Fat (0 g Mono, 0 g Poly, 0.5 g Sat); 5 mg Cholesterol; 3 g Carbohydrate (0 g Fibre, 0 g Sugar); 1 g Protein; 85 mg Sodium

Grilled Potato Skins

*Crispy and chewy, smoky and cheesy, potato skins done on the barbecue
disappear fast. Sour cream makes a great accompanying dip.*

Unpeeled medium baking potatoes	3	3
Cooking oil	2 tbsp.	30 mL
Chili powder	1 tsp.	5 mL
Ground coriander	1/2 tsp.	2 mL
Ground cumin	1/2 tsp.	2 mL
Salt	1/4 tsp.	1 mL
Pepper	1/4 tsp.	1 mL
Bacon slices, cooked crisp and crumbled	6	6
Grated Monterey Jack cheese	1/2 cup	125 mL
Grated sharp Cheddar cheese	1/2 cup	125 mL
Thinly sliced green onion	2 tbsp.	30 mL

With a fork, poke several holes randomly into potatoes. Microwave,
uncovered, on High for about 10 minutes, turning at halftime, until tender
(see Tip, below). Wrap in a tea towel and let stand for 5 minutes. Unwrap
and let stand for about 5 minutes until cool enough to handle. Cut potatoes
lengthwise into quarters. Scoop out pulp, leaving 1/4 inch (6 mm) shells.
Save pulp for another use.

Combine next 6 ingredients in a small cup. Brush over both sides of shells.
Preheat barbecue to medium. Place shells, skin-side up, on greased grill.
Close lid and cook for 5 minutes. Turn over.

Sprinkle remaining 4 ingredients over top. Close lid and cook for about
3 minutes until cheese is melted. Makes 12 potato skins.

*1 potato skin: 120 Calories; 7 g Total Fat (2.5 g Mono, 1 g Poly, 2.5 g Sat); 15 mg Cholesterol;
10 g Carbohydrate (1 g Fibre, 0 g Sugar); 5 g Protein; 210 mg Sodium*

Tip: The microwaves used in our test kitchen are 900 watts—but
microwaves are sold in many different powers. You should be able to find
the wattage of yours by opening the door and looking for the mandatory
label. If your microwave is more than 900 watts, you may need to reduce
the cooking time. If it is less than 900 watts, you will probably need to
increase the cooking time.

Sweet Potato Balls

Deep-fried crispiness in these attractive tidbits makes them a great appetizer. Kids love them too!

Sweet potatoes, peeled and cut up	1 lb.	454 g
All-purpose flour	1/3 cup	75 mL
Cornstarch	2 tbsp.	30 mL
Brown sugar, packed	2 tbsp.	30 mL
Nutmeg	1/4 tsp.	1 mL
Salt, to taste		

Cooking oil, for deep-frying

Cook sweet potato in water in a medium saucepan until tender. Drain well and mash.

Combine flour, cornstarch, sugar, nutmeg and salt well in a small bowl. Add to potato and mash well. Shape into 1 1/2 inch (3.8 cm) balls.

Deep-fry, a few at a time, in 375°F (190°C) cooking oil for about 5 minutes until browned. Remove with a slotted spoon to paper towels to drain. Makes 24 balls.

1 ball: 50 Calories; 2.5 g Total Fat (1.5 g Mono, 0.5 g Poly, 0 g Sat); 0 mg Cholesterol; 7 g Carbohydrate (0 g Fibre, 2 g Sugar); 0 g Protein; 10 mg Sodium

Choose firm sweet potatoes that don't have cracks, bruises, soft spots or any obvious signs of decay. Avoid buying refrigerated ones, and don't store raw sweet potatoes in the fridge as cold storage may change their flavour. Store them in a dark, cool, ventilated place for about a week. Sweet potatoes can be frozen once cooked.

The Potato: The Root that Fed an Empire

The archeological record shows that potatoes originated and were first cultivated in the Andes of South America, most likely in areas of southern Peru and northern Bolivia. Peoples in the area were harvesting wild potatoes more than 10,000 years ago. From 3000 to 7000 years ago, potatoes were being cultivated as a crop throughout much of the Andes.

The Inca, in particular, made wide use of potatoes. Not only were they eaten fresh, they were also dehydrated and mashed into a substance called chuño, which was eaten as-is or added to soups and stews. Chuño could keep for several years. The Inca also used potatoes medicinally.

Spanish explorers took the potato back to Spain with them from South America in the 1570s. Despite its reputation in its homeland, the potato was not well received by Europeans, who initially viewed it with distaste and suspicion. It took nearly 200 years for the potato to spread across the continent. By the late 1700s and early 1800s, it was becoming a staple for peasants in many European countries, as well as in parts of Asia. By the early 1800s it also gained popularity in North America, having been brought back to the Americas by European explorers and settlers.

Today it is considered one of the five most important crops grown worldwide, along with rice, wheat, corn and sugar cane. More than 4500 edible potato varieties are cultivated worldwide, most of them from the Andes. Many of the potatoes that are grown in the Andes look nothing like the potatoes we see in our local supermarkets, but they have similar nutritional content and are cooked and eaten in the same ways as the potatoes we buy.

So what makes this humble little tuber so important? Aside from its nutritional value, the potato is extremely valuable because it is so easy to grow. Potato crops have a huge geographical range. They thrive in diverse habitats from mountains to rain forests, and from the fields of southern Chile all the way to Greenland. They also have a greater yield per hectare than cereal crops (from 2 to 4 times better, depending on the plant), and they require a less than 1/5 of the water that cereal crops need to grow.

Potatoes are also less prone to crop failure than cereal crops because the edible part of the plant grows underground. If cereal crops grow too big or are subject to high winds or turbulent weather, the stalks fall over and the plants die. Tubers, however, grow underground, supported by the surrounding earth, so they can grow larger without affecting the strength of the plant and are not as affected by tumultuous weather.

Wherever potato was introduced, incidences of widespread famine dropped, infant mortality declined, and fewer people died of malnutrition. You could say that the humble little spud helped fuel the growth of many nations. It is truly a food fit for an empire.

Potato Wheat Biscuits

Mashed potatoes give these biscuits a lighter texture than traditional whole wheat biscuits. Cheesy and wholesome, these biscuits are great on their own or served alongside chili or soup.

All-purpose flour	1 cup	250 mL
Whole wheat flour	3/4 cup	175 mL
Grated light sharp Cheddar cheese	1/2 cup	125 mL
Grated Parmesan cheese	2 tbsp.	30 mL
Baking powder	1 tbsp.	15 mL
Salt	1/2 tsp.	2 mL
Milk	2/3 cup	150 mL
Cooking oil	3 tbsp.	45 mL
Mashed potatoes	1 cup	250 mL
Grated light sharp Cheddar cheese	1/4 cup	60 mL

Stir first 6 ingredients together in a large bowl. Make a well in centre.

Combine milk, cooking oil and potato in a medium bowl, stirring until smooth. Pour into well and stir to form a soft ball. Turn out and knead 6 to 8 times on a lightly floured surface. Divide into 12 equal portions. Shape into round balls. Place in a greased 9 inch (23 cm) round cake pan. Bake in 425°F (220°C) oven for 15 minutes.

Sprinkle with second amount of Cheddar cheese. Bake for about 5 minutes until browned. Makes 12 biscuits.

1 biscuit: 140 Calories; 6 g Total Fat (2 g Mono, 1 g Poly, 1.5 g Sat); 5 mg Cholesterol; 17 g Carbohydrate (0 g Fibre, 1 g Sugar); 5 g Protein; 240 mg Sodium

Potato Buns

These filling buns have a slightly sweet flavour and a chewy texture. You can also make tray buns with this recipe; simply arrange 18 balls of dough, touching each other, in each of 2 greased 9 x 13 inch (23 x 33 cm) pans. The rising and cooking times remain the same.

Potatoes (about 1 medium), peeled and cut up	1/2 lb.	225 g
Water	2 cups	500 mL
Butter (or hard margarine)	1/2 cup	125 mL
Granulated sugar	1/2 cup	125 mL
Salt	1 tsp.	5 mL
All-purpose flour	2 cups	500 mL
Instant yeast (or 1/4 oz., 8 g, envelope)	2 1/2 tsp.	12 mL
Large egg, fork-beaten	1	1
All-purpose flour, approximately	4 cups	1 L

Cook potato in water in a medium saucepan until tender. Drain, reserving 1 1/3 cups (325 mL) potato water. Mash potato in saucepan.

Add reserved potato water, butter, sugar and salt. Heat, stirring, until butter is melted. Turn into a large bowl. Cool slightly. Mixture should still be quite hot, not lukewarm.

Add first amount of flour, yeast and egg. Beat for 2 minutes.

Work in enough of second amount of flour until dough pulls away from sides of bowl and is smooth and elastic. Turn out and knead on a floured surface for 5 minutes. Divide dough into 3 equal portions. Shape each portion into 12 balls. Arrange 1 inch (2.5 cm) apart in 2 greased 11 x 17 inch (28 x 43 cm) pans. Cover with a tea towel. Let stand in oven with light on and door closed for about 1 1/2 hours until almost doubled in size. Bake one pan at a time in 400°F (200°C) oven for 10 to 15 minutes until golden brown. Turn out onto racks to cool. Makes 3 dozen buns.

1 bun: 120 Calories; 3 g Total Fat (0.5 g Mono, 0 g Poly, 1.5 g Sat); 5 mg Cholesterol; 20 g Carbohydrate (1 g Fibre, 3 g Sugar); 2 g Protein; 85 mg Sodium

Brown Grain Bread

Molasses gives this bread a slightly sweet taste that pairs perfectly with baked beans or hearty soups.

All-purpose flour	1 cup	250 mL
Whole wheat flour	1 cup	250 mL
All-bran cereal	1/2 cup	125 mL
Rolled oats (not instant)	1/2 cup	125 mL
Granulated sugar	2 tbsp.	30 mL
Instant yeast (or 1/4 oz., 8 g, envelope)	2 1/2 tsp.	12 mL
Salt	2 tsp.	10 mL
Very warm water	2 cups	500 mL
Milk	1/4 cup	60 mL
Fancy (mild) molasses	1/3 cup	75 mL
Butter (or hard margarine)	1/4 cup	60 mL
Mashed potatoes	1 cup	250 mL
All-purpose flour, approximately	4 1/2 cups	1.1 L
Butter (or hard margarine), softened	2 tsp.	10 mL

Combine first 7 ingredients in a large bowl. Make a well in centre.

Add water, milk, molasses, first amount of butter and mashed potato. Heat, stirring, until very warm and butter is melted. Pour into well. Beat for 2 minutes.

Work in enough of second amount of all-purpose flour until dough pulls away from sides of bowl. Turn out and knead for 8 to 10 minutes on a floured surface until smooth and elastic. Place in a large greased bowl, turning once to grease top. Cover with a tea towel and let stand in oven with light on and door closed for about 1 1/4 hours until doubled in bulk. Punch dough down and divide in half. Shape into 2 loaves. Place in 2 greased 9 x 5 x 3 inch (23 x 12.5 x 7.5 cm) loaf pans. Cover with a tea towel. Let stand in oven with light on and door closed for about 45 minutes until doubled in size. Bake in 375°F (190°C) oven for 35 to 40 minutes. Cover with foil for last 10 minutes if tops brown too quickly. Turn out onto racks to cool.

Brush hot loaf tops with second amount of butter. Makes 2 loaves that cut into 12 slices each.

1 slice: 160 Calories; 1 g Total Fat (0 g Mono, 0 g Poly, 0 g Sat); 0 mg Cholesterol; 33 g Carbohydrate (3 g Fibre, 4 g Sugar); 4 g Protein; 220 mg Sodium

Sweet Potato Knots

These pretty "knotted" buns have savoury notes from the sage and a slightly sweet flavour from the sweet potato. You can also use canned sweet potatoes if you do not have any cooked sweet potato on hand.

All-purpose flour	2 cups	500 mL
Finely chopped fresh sage	1 tbsp.	15 mL
(or 3/4 tsp., 4 mL, dried)		
Envelope of instant yeast (1/4 oz., 8 g)	1	1
(or 2 1/4 tsp., 11 mL)		
Salt	1 tsp.	5 mL
Onion powder	1/2 tsp.	2 mL
Mashed cooked sweet potato	1/2 cup	125 mL
Water	1/2 cup	125 mL
Buttermilk (or soured milk,	1/4 cup	60 mL
see Tip, page 146)		
Liquid honey	2 tbsp.	30 mL
Butter (or hard margarine)	1 tbsp.	15 mL
Large egg, fork-beaten	1	1
All-purpose flour	1 cup	250 mL
All-purpose flour, approximately	2 tbsp.	30 mL
Butter (or hard margarine), melted	1 tbsp.	15 mL

Combine first 5 ingredients in a large bowl. Make a well in centre.

Combine next 5 ingredients in a small saucepan. Heat, stirring, on medium until very warm (see Tip, page 25). Add to well and stir gently.

Add egg. Mix until a soft, sticky dough forms.

Add second amount of flour. Mix until dough pulls away from side of bowl and is no longer sticky.

Turn out onto a lightly floured surface. Knead for 5 to 10 minutes until smooth and elastic, adding third amount of flour 1 tbsp. (15 mL) at a time, if necessary, to prevent sticking. Place in a greased extra-large bowl, turning once to grease top. Cover with greased waxed paper and a tea towel. Let stand in oven with light on and door closed for about 1 hour until doubled in bulk. Punch dough down. Turn out onto lightly floured surface and divide into 12 portions. Roll 1 portion into a 10 inch (25 cm) long rope. Shape into a simple knot. Place in a greased muffin cup. Repeat with remaining portions.

Brush with second amount of butter. Cover with greased waxed paper and a tea towel. Let stand in oven with light on and door closed for about 30 minutes until doubled in size. Bake in 350°F (175°C) oven for about 17 minutes until golden. Remove rolls from pan and place on a wire rack to cool. Makes 12 rolls.

1 roll: 150 Calories; 1.5 g Total Fat (0 g Mono, 0 g Poly, 0.5 g Sat); 5 mg Cholesterol; 31 g Carbohydrate (1 g Fibre, 3 g Sugar); 4 g Protein; 220 mg Sodium

Tip: When using yeast, it is important for the liquid to be at the correct temperature. If the liquid is too cool, the yeast will not activate properly. If the liquid is too hot, the yeast will be destroyed. For best results, follow the recommended temperatures as instructed on the package.

Green Onion Hotcakes

These little cakes are great for lunch with a dab of sour cream. For a tasty variation, try adding 1 cup (250 mL) of grated sharp Cheddar to the dry ingredients.

Mashed potatoes	1 cup	250 mL
Large egg, fork-beaten	1	1
Salt	1/2 tsp.	2 mL
Granulated sugar	2 tsp.	10 mL
Milk	1 cup	250 mL
Butter (or hard margarine), melted	1 tbsp.	15 mL
All-purpose flour	1 cup	250 mL
Baking powder	1 tbsp.	15 mL
Finely chopped green onion	1/4 cup	60 mL

Combine potato and egg in a medium bowl. Stir in salt, sugar, milk and butter.

Stir in flour, baking powder and green onion, adding a bit more milk if necessary to make a spoonable, but barely pourable, batter. Grease a medium frying pan with oil or cooking spray and heat over medium. Drop batter by tablespoonful (15 mL) into pan. Brown both sides. Makes 34 small hotcakes.

2 hotcakes: 50 Calories; 1 g Total Fat (0 g Mono, 0 g Poly, 0.5 g Sat); 5 mg Cholesterol; 9 g Carbohydrate (0 g Fibre, 1 g Sugar); 2 g Protein; 140 mg Sodium

Sweet Potato Loaf

This tasty loaf is dense and moist with just the right amount of spice. As a variation, try adding 1/2 cup (125 mL) of raisins or chopped walnuts when you add the spices.

Butter (or hard margarine), softened	1/2 cup	125 mL
Granulated sugar	1/4 cup	60 mL
Brown sugar, packed	1/4 cup	60 mL
Large eggs	2	2
Mashed sweet potatoes	1 cup	250 mL
Fancy (mild) molasses	1/4 cup	60 mL
Vanilla extract	1 tsp.	5 mL
All-purpose flour	2 cups	500 mL
Baking powder	1/2 tsp.	2 mL
Baking soda	1 tsp.	5 mL
Salt	1/2 tsp.	2 mL
Ground cinnamon	3/4 tsp.	4 mL
Ground nutmeg	1/2 tsp.	2 mL
Ground allspice	1/4 tsp.	1 mL

Cream butter and both sugars in a large bowl. Beat in eggs, 1 at a time. Stir in sweet potato, molasses and vanilla.

Stir remaining 7 ingredients together in a medium bowl. Add to potato mixture and stir just to moisten. Turn into a greased 9 x 5 x 3 inch (23 x 12.5 x 7.5 cm) loaf pan. Bake in 350°F (175°C) oven for 50 to 60 minutes, until a wooden pick inserted in centre comes out clean. Cuts into 16 slices.

1 slice: 160 Calories; 6 g Total Fat (1.5 g Mono, 0 g Poly, 3.5 g Sat); 15 mg Cholesterol; 25 g Carbohydrate (1 g Fibre, 10 g Sugar); 2 g Protein; 220 mg Sodium

Cinnamon Buns

These gorgeous treats rise beautifully into delicious, high buns. The mashed potato in the dough gives the buns a nice light texture.

Hot potato water (or hot water)	2 1/2 cups	625 mL
Mashed potatoes	1 cup	250 mL
Butter (or hard margarine)	1/2 cup	125 mL
Large eggs	2	2
Granulated sugar	1/2 cup	125 mL
Salt	1 1/2 tsp.	7 mL
All-purpose flour	3 1/2 cups	875 mL
Envelopes of instant yeast (1/4 oz., 8 g, each) (or 5 tsp., 25 mL)	2	2
All-purpose flour, approximately	4 cups	1 L
Butter (or hard margarine), softened	2/3 cup	150 mL
Ground cinnamon	2 tbsp.	30 mL
Brown sugar, packed	1 cup	250 mL
Icing (confectioner's) sugar	1 1/2 cups	375 mL
Butter (or hard margarine), softened	3 tbsp.	45 mL
Vanilla extract	1/2 tsp.	2 mL
Milk (or water)	3 tbsp.	45 mL

Beat first 6 ingredients in a large bowl until butter is melted.

Add first amount of flour and yeast. Beat for about 2 minutes.

Work in enough of second amount of flour until dough pulls away from sides of bowl. Turn out onto a floured surface and knead 8 to 10 minutes until smooth and elastic. Divide into 3 equal portions. Roll 1 portion at a time into a 9 x 12 inch (23 x 30 cm) rectangle.

Spread each rectangle with 1/3 of butter.

Mix cinnamon and brown sugar in a small bowl. Sprinkle 1/3 of mixture evenly over each rectangle. Roll up each from long side. Cut into twelve 1 inch (2.5 cm) slices. Arrange in 2 greased 9 x 13 inch (23 x 33 cm) pans. Cover with tea towels and let stand in oven with light on and door closed for about 1 hour until doubled in size. Bake one pan at a time in 375°F (190°C) oven for about 20 minutes until browned. Turn out on racks to cool slightly. Turn right side up to ice.

For the icing, beat remaining 4 ingredients in a small bowl until smooth, adding more icing sugar or milk as necessary to make a thin glaze. Spoon or drizzle over warm buns. Makes 3 dozen buns.

1 bun: 210 Calories; 7 g Total Fat (2 g Mono, 0 g Poly, 4.5 g Sat); 20 mg Cholesterol; 34 g Carbohydrate (1 g Fibre, 13 g Sugar); 3 g Protein; 150 mg Sodium

Doughnuts

A sweet cake doughnut with a trace of nutmeg. Running your potatoes through a ricer instead of mashing them will produce a lighter, fluffier donut.

Mashed potatoes	1/2 cup	125 mL
Buttermilk (or soured milk, see Tip, page 146)	3/4 cup	175 mL
Large eggs	2	2
Granulated sugar	3/4 cup	175 mL
Butter (or hard margarine), melted	1/4 cup	60 mL
Vanilla extract	1 tsp.	5 mL
All-purpose flour	3 7/8 cups	950 mL
Baking powder	1 tbsp.	15 mL
Baking soda	1 tsp.	5 mL
Ground nutmeg	1/2 tsp.	2 mL
Ground cinnamon	1/4 tsp.	1 mL

Cooking oil, for deep-frying

Beat first 6 ingredients in a large bowl.

Stir flour, baking powder, baking soda, nutmeg and cinnamon together in a medium bowl. Add to potato mixture, stirring to moisten. Dough will be thick. Roll dough out a scant 1/2 inch (12 mm) thick on a lightly floured surface. Cut with a doughnut cutter.

Deep-fry 2 or 3 doughnuts at a time in 375°F (190°C) cooking oil until golden brown on both sides. Remove with a slotted spoon to paper towels to drain. Deep-fry "holes." Remove with a slotted spoon to paper towels to drain. Makes 18 doughnuts and 18 "holes."

1 doughnut: 190 Calories; 6 g Total Fat (2.5 g Mono, 1 g Poly, 2 g Sat); 10 mg Cholesterol; 31 g Carbohydrate (1 g Fibre, 9 g Sugar); 3 g Protein; 150 mg Sodium

To make sugared doughnuts, pour 1/3 cup (75 mL) granulated sugar into a plastic bag. Add 2 or 3 cooled doughnuts at a time and shake to coat. For cinnamon doughnuts, combine 1/4 tsp. (1 mL) cinnamon and 1/3 cup (75 mL) sugar in a plastic bag. Add 2 or 3 cooled doughnuts at a time and shake to coat.

Pot Roast Soup

This rich, stew-like soup is full of tender meat and vegetables, the perfect comfort food for a blustery fall or winter day.

Cooking oil	2 tsp.	10 mL
Beef top sirloin steak, trimmed of fat and diced	1 lb.	454 g
Chopped onion	1 cup	250 mL
Garlic cloves, minced (or 1/2 tsp., 2 mL, powder)	2	2
Prepared beef broth	5 cups	1.25 L
Cubed peeled potato	2 cups	500 mL
Baby carrots, halved	1 cup	250 mL
Tomato paste (see Tip, page 35)	1 tbsp.	15 mL
Worcestershire sauce	1 tbsp.	15 mL
Dried thyme	1/4 tsp.	1 mL
Salt	1/4 tsp.	1 mL
Water	1/4 cup	60 mL
All-purpose flour	1/4 cup	60 mL
Frozen peas	1 cup	250 mL

Heat cooking oil in a large saucepan on medium-high. Add beef and cook for about 10 minutes, stirring often, until browned. Reduce heat to medium.

Add onion and garlic. Cook for 3 to 5 minutes, stirring occasionally, until onion is softened.

Stir in beef broth and bring to a boil. Reduce heat to medium-low. Simmer, partially covered, for about 40 minutes until beef is tender.

Add next 6 ingredients. Bring to a boil.

Stir water into flour in a small bowl until smooth. Slowly add to soup, stirring constantly, until boiling and thickened. Reduce heat to medium. Boil gently, covered, for 15 to 20 minutes, stirring occasionally, until vegetables are tender.

Add peas. Heat, stirring, for 3 to 5 minutes until peas are tender. Makes 6 servings.

1 serving: 290 Calories; 9 g Total Fat (4 g Mono, 1 g Poly, 3 g Sat); 35 mg Cholesterol; 25 g Carbohydrate (4 g Fibre, 7 g Sugar); 21 g Protein; 740 mg Sodium

Tip: If a recipe calls for less than an entire can of tomato paste, freeze the unopened can for 30 minutes. Open both ends and push the contents through one end. Slice off only what you need and freeze the remaining paste in a resealable freezer bag or plastic wrap for future use.

Jazzy Jerk Soup

Tender pork and diced vegetables add a great deal of substance to this spicy soup. Although it takes a little time to prepare, the results are worth it! Serve with ciabatta bread or hot cornbread.

Cooking oil	2 tbsp.	30 mL
Boneless pork loin chops, cut into	1 lb.	454 g
1/2 inch (12 mm) thick slices		
Finely grated ginger root	1 tbsp.	15 mL
(or 3/4 tsp., 4 mL, ground ginger)		
Paprika	2 tsp.	10 mL
Salt	1 1/2 tsp.	7 mL
Dried crushed chilies	3/4 tsp.	4 mL
Dried thyme	1/2 tsp.	2 mL
Ground cinnamon	1/4 tsp.	1 mL
Ground allspice	1/8 tsp.	0.5 mL
Coarsely ground pepper, to taste		
Ground cloves, to taste		
Chopped onion	1 cup	250 mL
Garlic clove, minced	1	1
(or 1/4 tsp., 1 mL, powder)		
Prepared chicken broth	1 cup	250 mL
Prepared chicken broth	3 cups	750 mL
Diced peeled potato	2 cups	500 mL
Diced peeled sweet potato	2 cups	500 mL
Diced yellow turnip	2 cups	500 mL
Can of cream-style corn (14 oz., 398 mL)	1	1
Can of stewed tomatoes (14 oz., 398 mL),	1	1
with juice, coarsely chopped (see Tip)		
Sliced carrot	1 cup	250 mL
Coarsely shredded fresh spinach leaves,	2 cups	500 mL
lightly packed		

Heat cooking oil in a large frying pan on medium-high. Add next 10 ingredients. Cook for about 10 minutes, stirring occasionally, until pork is browned.

Add onion and garlic. Cook for 2 minutes, stirring occasionally. Stir in first amount of broth, scraping any brown bits from bottom of pan. Transfer to 4 to 5 quart (4 to 5 L) slow cooker.

Stir in next 7 ingredients. Cook, covered, on Low for 7 to 8 hours or on High for 3 1/2 to 4 hours.

Stir in spinach and cook, covered, on High for about 5 minutes until spinach is wilted. Makes about 12 cups (3 L).

1 cup (250 mL): 190 Calories; 7 g Total Fat (3 g Mono, 1 g Poly, 1.5 g Sat); 25 mg Cholesterol; 22 g Carbohydrate (3 g Fibre, 7 g Sugar); 11 g Protein; 740 mg Sodium

Tip: Cut tomatoes with a paring knife or kitchen shears while they are still in the can.

Baked Potato Soup

If you like your baked potato with all the fixings, you'll adore this soup.

Cooking oil	1 1/2 tsp.	7 mL
Chopped onion	1/2 cup	125 mL
Diced carrot	1/2 cup	125 mL
Chopped celery	1/2 cup	125 mL
Chicken stock	4 cups	1 L
Diced peeled potato	4 cups	1 L
Dill weed	1/4 tsp.	1 mL
Pepper	1/4 tsp.	1 mL
Bacon slices, cooked crisp and crumbled	8	8
Grated medium Cheddar cheese	1/2 cup	125 mL
Chopped green onion, as a garnish		

Heat cooking oil in a large saucepan on medium. Add next 3 ingredients and cook for 5 to 10 minutes, stirring often, until onion is softened.

Stir in next 4 ingredients and bring to a boil. Reduce heat to medium-low. Simmer, uncovered, for 10 to 15 minutes, stirring occasionally, until potato is tender.

Stir in bacon. Sprinkle cheese and green onion on individual servings. Makes 4 servings.

1 serving: 310 Calories; 13 g Total Fat (5 g Mono, 1 g Poly, 5 g Sat); 30 mg Cholesterol; 32 g Carbohydrate (3 g Fibre, 5 g Sugar); 16 g Protein; 950 mg Sodium

Potato Sausage Soup

This hearty soup has a nice spicy kick thanks to the paprika and pepperoni. Serve with fresh crusty bread, and garnish with croutons and fresh herbs.

Peeled, cubed potatoes	3 cups	750 mL
Medium onion, chopped	1	1
Paprika	2 tsp.	10 mL
Ground marjoram	1/2 tsp.	2 mL
Salt	1/2 tsp.	2 mL
Pepper	1/4 tsp.	1 mL
Garlic powder	1/4 tsp.	1 mL
Prepared beef broth	2 cups	500 mL
Sliced pepperoni	1/2 cup	125 mL
Water	2 cups	500 mL
Light sour cream, optional		

Cook first 8 ingredients in a large saucepan for about 20 minutes until vegetables are tender. Do not drain. Mash well.

Add pepperoni and remaining water. Simmer for 5 minutes.

Top individual servings with a dollop of sour cream, if using. Makes 5 cups (1.25 L).

1 cup (250 mL): 150 Calories; 5 g Total Fat (2.5 g Mono, 0 g Poly, 2.5 g Sat); 15 mg Cholesterol; 20 g Carbohydrate (2 g Fibre, 2 g Sugar); 6 g Protein; 670 mg Sodium

Only Chicken Soup

It's not a lie—everything but the chicken is blended smooth! This creamy, golden soup has a wonderful medley of vegetable and chicken flavours.

Chopped onion	1 cup	250 mL
Chopped celery	1 cup	250 mL
Garlic clove, minced	1	1
(or 1/4 tsp., 1 mL, powder)		
Cooking oil	1 tbsp.	15 mL
Prepared chicken broth	6 cups	1.5 L
Chopped carrot (about 2 medium)	1 cup	250 mL
Medium potatoes, peeled and cut	2	2
into 8 chunks		
Peeled diced zucchini	1 1/2 cups	375 mL
Boneless, skinless chicken breast	8 oz.	225 g
halves (about 2)		
Parsley flakes	2 tsp.	10 mL
Bay leaf	1	1
Alphabet pasta, uncooked (optional)	1/2 cup	125 mL

Sauté onion, celery and garlic in cooking oil in a large uncovered pot or Dutch oven until onion is soft and clear.

Stir in remaining 8 ingredients. Simmer, covered, for 1 hour. Remove chicken to a cutting board. Remove and discard bay leaf. Purée soup, in 2 batches, in a blender or with a hand blender until smooth, following manufacturer's directions for processing hot liquids. Return to pot. Cut chicken into bite-sized pieces and return to soup. Makes 10 2/3 cups (2.7 L).

1 cup (250 mL): 100 Calories; 1.5 g Total Fat (1 g Mono, 0 g Poly, 0 g Sat); 10 mg Cholesterol; 14 g Carbohydrate (1 g Fibre, 3 g Sugar); 8 g Protein; 410 mg Sodium

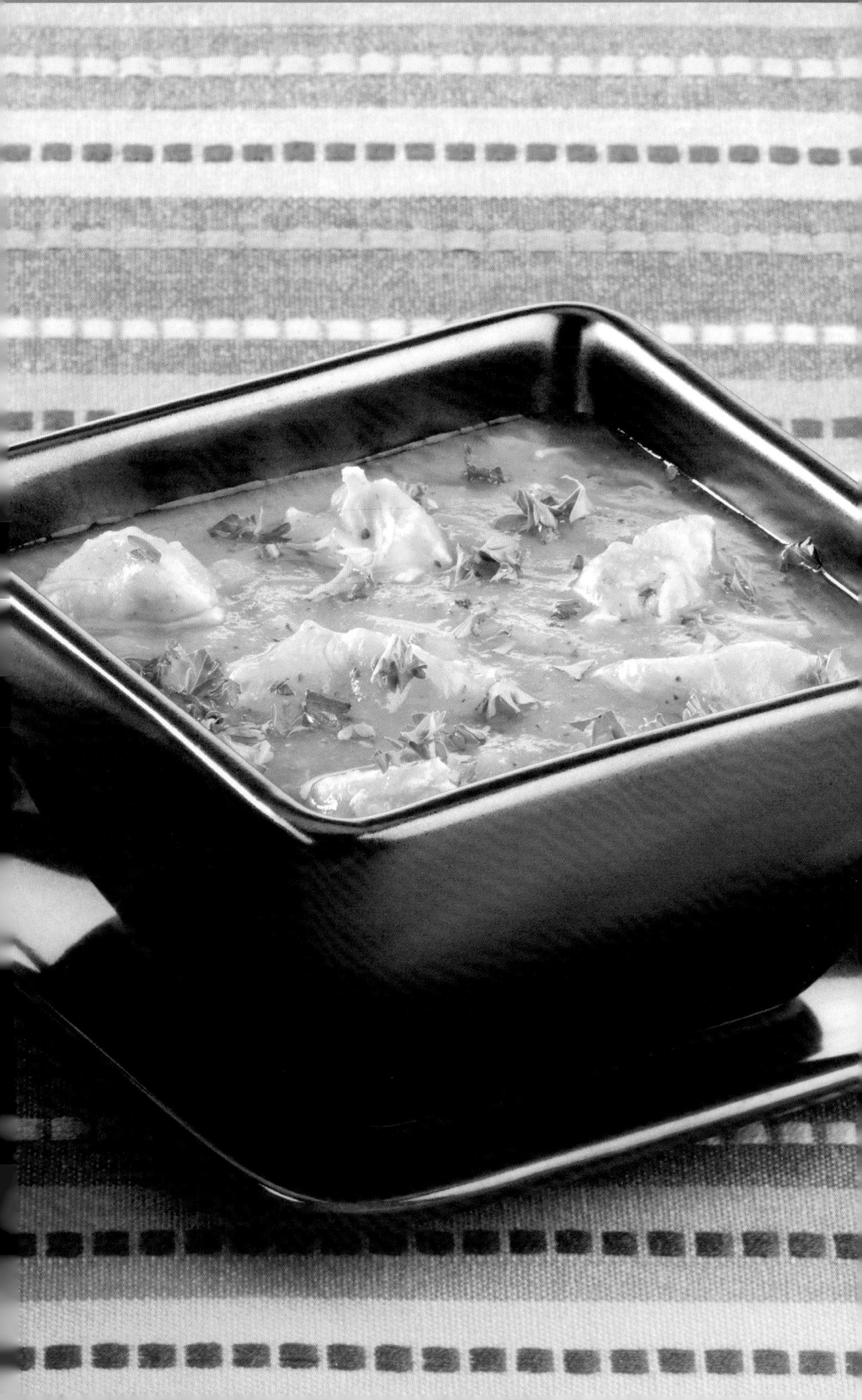

Spicy Sweet Potato Soup

This lovely, autumn soup is loaded with sweet potato and corn. Increase the cayenne pepper if you'd like more heat.

Butter (or hard margarine)	2 tbsp.	30 mL
Thinly sliced onion	2 cups	500 mL
Garlic cloves, minced	4	4
Paprika	2 tsp.	10 mL
Ground coriander	1 tsp.	5 mL
Cayenne pepper	1/4 tsp.	1 mL
Sweet potato, peeled and cut into 1 1/2 inch (3.8 cm) cubes (about 5 cups, 1.25 L)	2 lbs.	900 g
Prepared chicken broth	8 cups	2 L
Can of kernal corn (14 oz., 398 mL)	1	1
Pepper, sprinkle		
Sour cream, for garnish	1/4 cup	60 mL
Chopped fresh chives, for garnish	1/4 cup	60 mL

Melt butter in a large pot or Dutch oven on medium. Add onion and cook, uncovered, for 5 to 10 minutes, stirring often, until softened.

Add next 4 ingredients. Heat, stirring, for 1 to 2 minutes until fragrant.

Add sweet potato and toss until coated.

Stir in broth and bring to a boil. Reduce heat to medium-low. Simmer, covered, for 25 to 30 minutes, stirring occasionally, until sweet potato is tender. Remove from heat. Let stand for 5 minutes. Process sweet potato mixture, in 2 batches, in a blender or food processor until smooth, following manufacturer's instructions for processing hot liquids. Return to same pot.

Stir in corn and pepper. Bring to a boil on medium-high. Heat, stirring, for 3 to 4 minutes until heated through.

Ladle soup into 8 individual bowls. Swirl a dollop of sour cream through centre of each. Sprinkle chives over top. Makes 8 cups (2 L).

1 cup (250 mL): 220 Calories; 4.5 g Total Fat (1 g Mono, 0 g Poly, 3 g Sat); 10 mg Cholesterol; 39 g Carbohydrate (5 g Fibre, 11 g Sugar); 7 g Protein; 900 mg Sodium

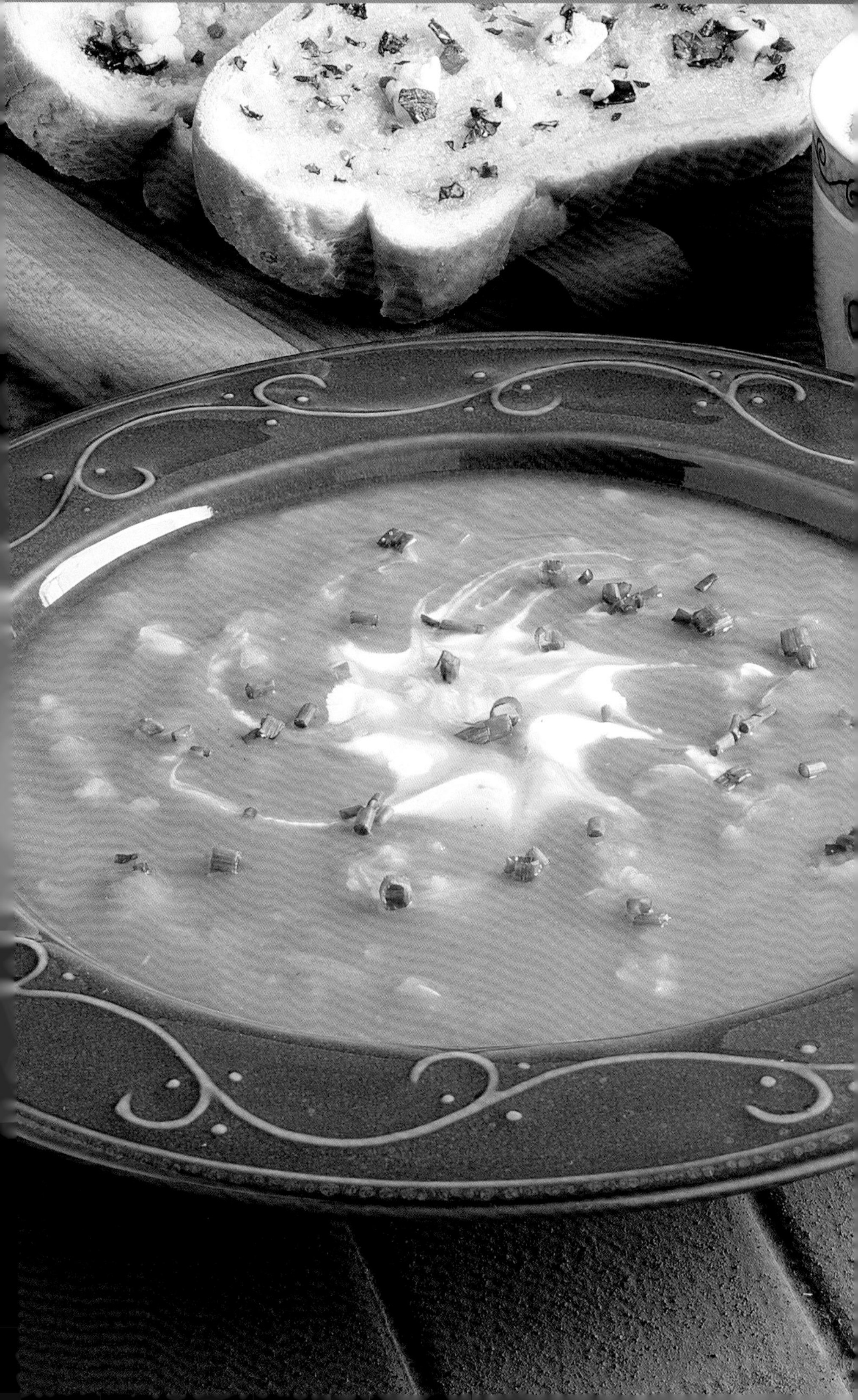

Basa Bisque

Though people often expect shellfish to be the base ingredient in bisques, this version uses basa instead. We've also used evaporated milk as a lower-fat alternative to the traditional cream.

Cooking oil	1 tsp.	5 mL
Chopped onion	1 cup	250 mL
Chopped celery	1/2 cup	125 mL
Garlic cloves, minced	2	2
(or 1/2 tsp., 2 mL, powder)		
Water	2 1/2 cups	625 mL
Chopped peeled potatoes	2 cups	500 mL
Yellow (or green) wax beans, quartered	1 1/2 cups	375 mL
Chopped carrot	1 cup	250 mL
Frozen kernel corn	1/2 cup	125 mL
Bay leaf	1	1
Can of evaporated milk (13 1/2 oz., 385 mL)	1	1
Milk	1 cup	250 mL
All-purpose flour	1/4 cup	60 mL
Salt	1 1/2 tsp.	7 mL
Pepper	1/2 tsp.	2 mL
Ground nutmeg	1/8 tsp.	0.5 mL
Basa fillets, any small bones removed,	1 lb.	454 g
cut into 1 inch (2.5 cm) pieces		

Heat cooking oil in a Dutch oven on medium. Add next 3 ingredients. Cook for 5 to 10 minutes, stirring often, until onion is softened.

Stir in next 6 ingredients and bring to a boil. Reduce heat to medium-low. Simmer, covered, for about 20 minutes, stirring occasionally, until vegetables are soft.

Whisk next 6 ingredients in a small bowl until smooth. Add to vegetables and heat on medium, stirring constantly, until boiling and slightly thickened.

Add fish. Simmer for 5 minutes, stirring occasionally, until fish flakes easily when tested with a fork. Remove and discard bay leaf. Carefully process, in 3 batches, in a blender or with a hand blender until smooth, following manufacturer's instructions for processing hot liquids. Makes about 9 1/4 cups (2.3 L).

1 cup (250 mL): 150 Calories; 2 g Total Fat (0 g Mono, 0 g Poly, 1 g Sat); 5 mg Cholesterol; 21 g Carbohydrate (2 g Fibre, 6 g Sugar); 13 g Protein; 660 mg Sodium

Potato Broccoli Soup

This soup is equally delicious whether it is puréed smooth or left chunky. Garnish with a broccoli floret or some chopped green onion for a nice presentation.

Medium onions, chopped	2	2
Garlic clove, minced (or 1/4 tsp., 1 mL, powder), optional	1	1
Butter (or margarine)	1 tbsp.	15 mL
Peeled diced potato	4 cups	1 L
Chopped broccoli	4 cups	1 L
Salt	1 tsp.	5 mL
Pepper	1/4 tsp.	1 mL
Prepared vegetable broth	6 cups	1.5 L
Can of skim evaporated milk (13 1/2 oz., 385 mL)	1	1
Grated light sharp Cheddar cheese	1/2 cup	125 mL

Sauté onion and garlic in butter in a large saucepan or Dutch oven for about 10 minutes until onion is soft and starting to turn golden.

Add next 5 ingredients. Bring to a boil and cook until potatoes are tender.

Stir in milk. For a smooth soup, purée soup in a blender or with a hand blender until smooth, following manufacturer's instructions for processing hot liquids. For a chunky soup, transfer some solids with a slotted spoon to a small bowl. Purée remainder of soup in a blender or with a hand blender until smooth, and return solids to saucepan.

Sprinkle individual servings with grated cheese. Makes 10 3/4 cups (2.7 L).

1 cup (250 mL): 130 Calories; 3 g Total Fat (0 g Mono, 0 g Poly, 2 g Sat); 5 mg Cholesterol; 20 g Carbohydrate (1 g Fibre, 5 g Sugar); 6 g Protein; 840 mg Sodium

Vichyssoise

This classic, elegant soup is surprisingly easy to make and uses common ingredients that you most likely have on hand in your pantry. It is the perfect summer soup, cold, creamy and refreshing.

Peeled, cubed potatoes	4 cups	1 L
Leeks (white part only), cut up	3	3
Medium onion, sliced	1	1
Parsley flakes	1 tsp.	5 mL
Salt	1 tsp.	5 mL
Pepper	1/4 tsp.	1 mL
Ground nutmeg	1/8 tsp.	0.5 mL
Prepared vegetable broth	3 cups	750 mL
Water	1 3/4 cups	425 mL
Skim evaporated milk (or light cream)	2/3 cup	150 mL
Milk	1 cup	250 mL

Chopped chives, for garnish

Combine first 9 ingredients in a large saucepan. Cook until vegetables are tender. Purée soup in a blender or with a hand blender until smooth, following manufacturer's instructions for processing hot liquids. Pour into a large bowl.

Stir in both milks. Chill, covered, for several hours.

Sprinkle chives on top. Makes 8 cups (2 L).

1 cup (250 mL): 125 Calories; 1 g Total Fat (0 g Mono, 0 g Poly, 0.5 g Sat); 0 mg Cholesterol; 25 g Carbohydrate (2 g Fibre, 6 g Sugar); 5 g Protein; 700 mg Sodium

German Potato Salad

This potato salad has a vinegar and sugar base in place of mayonnaise and is loaded with plenty of bacon and onion. Scrumptious! German potato salads can be served warm or cold, but we think this recipe tastes best when served warm.

Waxy potatoes (about 4 medium), peeled and quartered	2 lbs.	900 g
Salt	3/4 tsp.	4 mL
Pepper	1/8 tsp.	0.5 mL
Bacon slices, diced	6	6
Chopped onion	1 cup	250 mL
Granulated sugar	1 1/2 tbsp.	22 mL
All-purpose flour	1 tbsp.	15 mL
Dry mustard	1/2 tsp.	2 mL
Salt	1/8 tsp.	0.5 mL
Milk	1/2 cup	125 mL
White vinegar	1 1/2 tbsp.	22 mL
Chopped fresh parsley	2 tsp.	30 mL

Cook potato in water in a large saucepan until tender. Drain and set aside until cool enough to handle. Cut into small cubes or dice.

Add first amount of salt and pepper and toss until potato is evenly coated. Cover to keep warm (see Tip, below).

Cook bacon in a frying pan for 3 to 4 minutes. Add onion and fry until onion is golden. Drain. Stir into potato and cover to keep warm.

Mix sugar, flour, mustard and second amount of salt in a small saucepan.

Stir in milk and vinegar until smooth. Heat, stirring, until boiling and thickened. Pour over potato mixture. Toss gently to coat. Sprinkle with parsley. Makes 4 cups (1 L).

3/4 cup (175 mL): 350 Calories; 18 g Total Fat (8 g Mono, 2 g Poly, 6 g Sat); 30 mg Cholesterol; 37 g Carbohydrate (3 g Fibre, 7 g Sugar); 9 g Protein; 720 mg Sodium

Tip: To keep potatoes warm, put them in a 200°F (95°C) oven for a short time. Potato dishes may be reheated in a 350°F (175°C) oven until hot.

Two-Potato Black Bean Salad

This is not your typical potato salad. In this dish, South American-inspired flavours are united by a spicy citrus vinaigrette. Delicious!

Cubed fresh peeled orange-fleshed sweet potato (1 inch, 2.5 cm, pieces)	3 cups	750 mL
Cubed peeled potato (1 inch, 2.5 cm, pieces)	1 1/2 cups	375 mL
Chopped red pepper (1 inch, 2.5 cm, pieces)	1 cup	250 mL
Cooking oil	1 tbsp.	15 mL
Salt	1/4 tsp.	1 mL
Pepper	1/4 tsp.	1 mL
Can of black beans, rinsed and drained (19 oz., 540 mL)	1	1
Thinly sliced red onion	1/4 cup	60 mL
Chopped fresh cilantro (or parsley)	2 tbsp.	30 mL
Olive (or cooking) oil	1/4 cup	60 mL
Lime juice	2 tbsp.	30 mL
Red wine vinegar	1 tbsp.	15 mL
Finely chopped chipotle peppers in adobo sauce (see Tip, below)	1 tsp.	5 mL
Granulated sugar	1 tsp.	5 mL
Salt	1/2 tsp.	2 mL
Grated lime zest	1/4 tsp.	1 mL
Small garlic clove, minced (or 1/8 tsp., 0.5 mL, powder)	1	1

Combine first 6 ingredients in a large bowl. Arrange in a single layer on a greased baking sheet with sides. Bake in 375°F (190°C) oven for about 30 minutes until tender. Return to same large bowl. Set aside to cool.

Add next 3 ingredients.

For the vinaigrette, whisk remaining 8 ingredients in a small bowl. Drizzle over potato mixture and toss well. Makes about 6 cups (1.5 L).

1 cup (250 mL): 290 Calories; 13 g Total Fat (8 g Mono, 1.5 g Poly, 1.5 g Sat); 0 mg Cholesterol; 40 g Carbohydrate (8 g Fibre, 6 g Sugar); 9 g Protein; 530 mg Sodium

Tip: Chipotle peppers in adobo sauce are smoked jalapeño peppers that are canned in a smoky red sauce. Adobo sauce is not as spicy as the chipotle pepper, but it still packs some heat. Be sure to wash your hands after handling. Store leftover chipotle peppers with their sauce in an airtight container in the refrigerator for up to 1 year.

Steak and Potato Salad

Toss your favourites on the grill to create this simple, appetizing salad!
A great meal for those hot summer days—no need for the oven.
Serve with garlic toast.

Fresh peeled potatoes, cubed	1 lb.	454 g
Water	1 tbsp.	15 mL
Montreal steak spice	2 tsp.	10 mL
Beef strip loin steak	1 lb.	454 g
Fresh asparagus, trimmed of tough ends	1 lb.	454 g
Balsamic vinaigrette dressing	3 tbsp.	45 mL
Spring mix, lightly packed	6 cups	1.5 L
Avocado, thinly sliced	1	1
Balsamic vinaigrette dressing	1/3 cup	75 mL
Shaved Parmesan cheese (optional)	1/2 cup	125 mL

Arrange potato slices in a single layer on a large microwave-safe plate. Sprinkle with water. Microwave, covered, on high (100%) for about 4 minutes until tender-crisp.

Sprinkle steak spice on both sides of steak. Preheat gas barbecue to medium-high. Cook steak on a greased grill for about 4 minutes per side until internal temperature reaches 145°F (63°C) for medium-rare or until steak reaches desired doneness. Transfer to a cutting board and cover with foil. Let stand for 10 minutes. Slice thinly. Transfer to an extra-large bowl.

Reduce heat to medium. Brush potato and asparagus with first amount of dressing. Cook on a greased grill for 8 to 10 minutes, turning occasionally, until browned and tender. Transfer to a cutting board. Let stand until cool enough to handle. Cut into 1 inch (2.5 cm) pieces. Add to steak.

Toss in next 3 ingredients. Sprinkle with cheese. Makes about 14 cups (3.5 L).

1 1/2 cups (375 mL): 210 Calories; 10 g Total Fat (2 g Mono, 0 g Poly, 3 g Sat); 30 mg Cholesterol; 15 g Carbohydrate (3 g Fibre, 5 g Sugar); 15 g Protein; 440 mg Sodium

Herbed Potato Salad

A little bit of green makes this avocado and smoky bacon potato salad a unique picnic treat. Pairs wonderfully with chicken and roasted veggies.

Mayonnaise	1/3 cup	75 mL
Chopped fresh chives	2 tbsp.	30 mL
Chopped fresh mint	2 tbsp.	30 mL
Chopped fresh parsley	2 tbsp.	30 mL
Dijon mustard	2 tbsp.	30 mL
Salt	1/8 tsp.	0.5 mL
Pepper, to taste		
Red potatoes, peeled and quartered	3 lbs.	1.4 kg
Bacon slices, cooked crisp and crumbled	4	4
Thinly sliced green onion	1/3 cup	75 mL
Ripe large avocado, chopped	1	1

Combine first 7 ingredients in a small bowl. Set aside.

Cook potato in boiling salted water in a large saucepan until just tender. Drain. Rinse with cold water and drain well. Cut into 1 inch (2.5 cm) pieces. Put into a large bowl.

Toss in bacon and green onion. Add mayonnaise mixture and toss until well coated.

Scatter avocado over top. Makes 6 servings.

1 serving: 360 Calories; 16 g Total Fat (10 g Mono, 3.5 g Poly, 2.5 g Sat); 10 mg Cholesterol; 44 g Carbohydrate (6 g Fibre, 2 g Sugar); 8 g Protein; 270 mg Sodium

Southern Potato Salad

Corn in a potato salad? You bet! Corn gives the salad a subtle sweetness, while the red pepper and onion provide a snappy crunch.

White vinegar	2 tbsp.	30 mL
Lemon juice	1 tbsp.	15 mL
Granulated sugar	1 tbsp.	15 mL
Cooking oil	2 tbsp.	30 mL
Chili powder	1 tsp.	5 mL
Salt	3/4 tsp.	4 mL
Pepper	1/4 tsp.	1 mL
Peeled, cooked, diced orange flesh sweet potatoes	4 cups	1 L
Sliced red onion	1/2 cup	125 mL
Chopped red pepper	1/3 cup	75 mL
Chopped cilantro	1 tbsp.	15 mL
Cooked frozen kernel (or canned, drained) corn	1 cup	250 mL

Combine first 7 ingredients in a medium bowl.

Add remaining 5 ingredients. Toss gently to coat well. Chill for 1 to 2 hours to blend flavours. Makes 5 cups (1.25 L).

1 cup (250 mL): 180 Calories; 6 g Total Fat (3.5 g Mono, 1.5 g Poly, 0 g Sat); 0 mg Cholesterol; 31 g Carbohydrate (3 g Fibre, 5 g Sugar); 3 g Protein; 370 mg Sodium

Potatoes: Friend or Foe?

Potatoes often get a bad rap as a "white," vegetable. Critics imply that they are devoid of nutrition, no more than empty calories. However, some white foods are actually nutritional powerhouses (remember the cauliflower craze?), and potatoes are no exception. The peoples of Peru and Ireland could not have sustained their families without these trusty tubers for countless generations, especially during times of famine, if potatoes were not highly nutritious.

An average medium-sized potato, regardless of the variety, has only about 150 calories and no fat, cholesterol or sodium. When you consider that the average person requires between 1800 and 2400 calories per day, depending on gender and level of activity, 150 calories seems pretty reasonable for an item as filling and as wholesome as the potato, especially when you consider what you are getting with those calories. Potatoes are high in fibre, which helps maintain digestive and colon health, promotes regularity and keeps you feeling fuller longer (which can also help with weight management). They are also an excellent source of vitamins and minerals, including vitamin C, an antioxidant that supports the immune system and helps prevent cell damage; as well as phosphorous and calcium, which are essential for strong, healthy bones; and the list goes on…protein, iron, magnesium, potassium, folate. Potatoes have them all.

Yes, they are high in carbohydrates, but your body *needs* carbs! They are not the enemy; they are fuel for your body!

The trick is to go easy on what you add to the potatoes. It's the fixin's that can turn a healthful potato into a heart attack on a plate. Some of the ingredients we add to potato dishes that make our taste buds so happy are not so friendly to the rest of our body. Sure a baked potato heaped with bacon, sour cream and cheese is delicious, but it's also a huge source of fat and calories that can be hard on the heart and waistline if it becomes an everyday indulgence. Choose healthier options on most days and save the fully loaded baked potato as a "sometimes food."

How you cook your potatoes also contributes to how good for you the final product will be. Boiled potatoes lose a lot of their nutrition to the water while cooking if they are peeled, so keep the skin on until after the potatoes are cooked. Roasting, baking and grilling are good options, as long as you use a minimal amount of oil. Stay away from the deep fryer if you are trying to keep things healthy. French fries are one of the tastiest ways to eat potatoes, but deep fried they are also one of the least healthy options. Try oven-baked fries instead, and jazz them up with herbs and spices instead of loads of salt.

Potatoes are the ultimate comfort food, and some of our favourite potato recipes are on the less-than-healthy side, but that doesn't mean they should be stricken from the menu. If you choose from the many delicious, satisfying and healthful potato recipes most of the time, you have plenty of room to pick a few recipes from the indulgence list as a special treat from time to time.

Meaty Roulade

Reminescent of a giant sausage roll and yet elegant enough to serve to company. Serve with a fresh garden salad on the side.

Finely chopped onion	1 cup	250 mL
Chopped fresh mushrooms	2 cups	500 mL
Butter (or margarine)	1 tbsp.	15 mL
Lean ground beef	1 lb.	454 g
Finely chopped red pepper	1/3 cup	75 mL
All-purpose flour	1/4 cup	60 mL
Salt	1 tsp.	5 mL
Pepper	1/4 tsp.	1 mL
Dried thyme	1/2 tsp.	2 mL
Light sour cream	1/2 cup	125 mL
Light cream cheese, softened	4 oz.	125 g
Large egg	1	1
Mashed potatoes	1 cup	250 mL
Salt	1/2 tsp.	2 mL
Package of fozen puff pastry (14.1 oz., 397 g), thawed according to package directions	1	1

Sauté onion and mushrooms in butter in a medium frying pan until onion is golden. Transfer to a small bowl.

Add ground beef and red pepper to same frying pan. Scramble-fry until no pink remains in beef. Drain.

Sprinkle with flour, salt, pepper and thyme. Mix well. Add sour cream and stir until thickened. Stir in mushroom mixture and set aside.

Beat cream cheese and egg together in a large bowl until smooth. Add potatoes and salt. Mix well.

Roll 1 square of puff pastry to 15 inch (38 cm) square. Spread 1/2 of potato mixture along bottom 1/3 of pastry, about 1 inch (2.5 cm) from edges. Spread 1/2 of meat mixture on top of potato mixture. Roll up from side with potato like a jelly roll. Roll slightly to seal edges. Pinch to seal sides. Place seam side down on an ungreased baking sheet. Cut slits decoratively in top to allow steam to escape. Repeat with remaining filling and pastry. Bake in 400°F (200°C) oven for 35 to 40 minutes until golden brown and crisp. Makes 8 servings.

1 serving: 500 Calories; 30 g Total Fat (15 g Mono, 3 g Poly, 10 g Sat); 45 mg Cholesterol; 34 g Carbohydrate (2 g Fibre, 3 g Sugar); 19 g Protein; 710 mg Sodium

Moussaka

Although it is typically considered a Greek dish, moussaka may actually be of Arabic origin. Eggplant, an integral ingredient in the dish, was unknown in Greece and the Mediterranneran region until the Arabs introduced it to the area in the Middle Ages. Today, many countries throughout southeastern Europe and the Middle East have their own versions of moussaka, each with their own regional variations in name and ingredients. Even within Greece there are many versions of this beloved dish. We prefer this version, which includes a generous layer of potato under the famous bechamel topping.

Unpeeled medium eggplant, cut into 1/2 inch (12 mm) slices	1	1
Salt	1 tsp.	5 mL
Potatoes, (about 4 medium), peeled and cut into 1/2 inch (12 mm) slices	2 lbs.	900 g
Lean ground lamb (or beef)	1 1/2 lbs.	680 g
Chopped onion	1 cup	250 mL
Salt	1 tsp.	5 mL
Pepper	1/2 tsp.	2 mL
Ground thyme	1/8 tsp.	0.5 mL
Ground nutmeg	1/8 tsp.	0.5 mL
Ground cinnamon	1/8 tsp.	0.5 mL
Garlic powder	1/4 tsp.	1 mL
Can of tomatoes (14 oz., 398 mL), with juice, broken up	1	1
Butter (not margarine)	1/4 cup	60 mL
All-purpose flour	1/4 cup	60 mL
Milk, warmed	3 cups	750 mL
Salt	1/4 tsp.	1 mL
Ground nutmeg	1/4 tsp.	1 mL
Grated part-skim mozzarella cheese	1 cup	250 mL
Grated light sharp Cheddar cheese	1/2 cup	125 mL

Season both sides of eggplant slices with salt and pepper and place them on a rack placed on a baking sheet. Let stand for at least 30 minutes. Rinse eggplant slices well to wash off salt. Drain well, squeezing out excess water if necessary, and pat dry. Arrange slices on a greased baking sheet with sides. Broil on top rack of oven for 4 to 5 minutes per side until browned and softened.

Cook potato in salted water in a large saucepan until just tender. Don't overcook. Drain well.

Scramble-fry ground lamb and onion in a non-stick frying pan until brown. Drain.

For the bechamel sauce, melt butter in a medium saucepan on medium-low. Add flour and whisk to form a paste. Add warm milk, 1/2 cup (25 mL) at a time, whisking constantly until mixture is smooth and all milk is incorporated. Whisk in second amount of salt and nutmeg. Cook on medium heat, stirring often, for about 12 minutes, until simmering and thickened. Remove from heat.

Add next 7 ingredients to lamb mixture and stir well. Layer eggplant in bottom of a greased 9 x 13 inch (23 x 33 cm) pan. Spread 1/2 of lamb mixture on top. Cover with potato slices, overlapping. Top with remaining 1/2 of meat mixture. Pour bechamel sauce overtop and smooth out with a spatula.

Sprinkle with mozzarella, then Cheddar cheese. Bake in 350°F (175°C) oven for 40 to 45 minutes until heated through and cheese is melted. Makes 8 servings.

1 serving: *395 Calories; 15 g Total Fat (3.5 g Mono, 1 g Poly, 8 g Sat); 85 mg Cholesterol; 37 g Carbohydrate (5 g Fibre, 10 g Sugar); 29 g Protein; 850 mg Sodium*

Beef and Sweet Potato Ragout

Sweet potato adds an unexpected depth to this rich-tasting, red wine-enhanced stew. Serve with egg noodles or rice.

Beef top sirloin steak, trimmed of fat	1 lb.	454 g
Seasoned salt	1/2 tsp.	2 mL
Pepper	1/4 tsp.	1 mL
Canola oil	1 tsp.	5 mL
Sliced fresh white mushrooms	2 cups	500 mL
Chopped onion	1/2 cup	125 mL
Garlic cloves, minced,	2	2
(or 1/2 tsp., 2 mL, powder)		
Dried rosemary, crushed	3/4 tsp.	4 mL
Cubed sweet potato	2 cups	500 mL
Prepared beef broth	1 cup	250 mL
Dry (or alcohol-free) red wine	1/2 cup	125 mL
Dijon mustard	2 tbsp.	30 mL
Worcestershire sauce	1 tsp.	5 mL
All-purpose flour	1 tbsp.	15 mL

Cut steak in half lengthwise. Cut halves crosswise into 1/4 inch (6 mm) thick slices, about 3 inches (7.5 cm) long. Sprinkle with seasoned salt and pepper. Heat canola oil in a large frying pan on medium-high. Add beef and cook for 2 to 3 minutes, stirring often, until desired doneness. Transfer to a plate and cover to keep warm.

Add next 4 ingredients to same frying pan. Cook, stirring, for 3 to 5 minutes until onion starts to soften.

Stir in next 5 ingredients and bring to a boil. Reduce heat to medium. Cook, covered, for about 8 minutes until sweet potato is tender.

Stir 2 tbsp. (30 mL) cooking liquid into flour in a small cup until smooth. Add to sweet potato mixture. Heat, stirring, until boiling and thickened. Add beef and cook, stirring, until heated through. Makes 4 servings.

1 serving: 360 Calories; 11 g Total Fat (5 g Mono, 1 g Poly, 4 g Sat); 55 mg Cholesterol; 21 g Carbohydrate (3 g Fibre, 5 g Sugar); 25 g Protein; 550 mg Sodium

Tourtière Turnovers

A true French-Canadian classic with a twist! Instead of the traditional pie form, this tourtière comes in it's own little hand-held package. Makes a great appetizer or offering at a potluck or buffet.

Lean ground pork	1/2 lb.	225 g
Finely chopped onion	1/3 cup	75 mL
Peeled, diced potato	2 cups	500 mL
Parsley flakes	1 tsp.	5 mL
Dried savory leaves	1/2 tsp.	2 mL
Celery salt	1/4 tsp.	1 mL
Salt	1 tsp.	5 mL
Pepper	1/4 tsp.	1 mL
Ground nutmeg	1/8 tsp.	0.5 mL
Bay leaf	1	1
Water	1 cup	250 mL

Pastry for a 2 crust pie, your own or a mix

Large egg, fork-beaten	1	1
Milk	1 tbsp.	15 mL

Combine first 11 ingredients in a large saucepan. Heat on medium-high, stirring frequently, until boiling. Reduce heat to medium-low. Cook, covered, for 45 minutes until liquid has absorbed and potatoes are very soft. Discard bay leaf. Stir until mixture is smooth. Set aside to cool.

Roll 1/4 of pastry thinly into 8 x 8 inch (20 x 20 cm) rectangle on a floured surface. Cut into four 4 x 4 inch (10 x 10 cm) squares. Place about 2 1/2 tbsp. (37 mL) filling to one side of centre on diagonal of each square.

Beat egg and milk together in a small dish. Brush 2 adjoining edges of filling side of pastry with egg wash to moisten. Fold unmoistened side diagonally over filling. Crimp to seal. Repeat with remaining pastry and filling. Cut slits in top of pastry. Brush with egg wash. Bake on an ungreased baking sheet in 375°F (190°C) oven for 40 minutes until golden brown. Makes 16 turnovers.

1 turnover: 125 Calories; 7 g Total Fat (2.5 g Mono, 0.5 g Poly, 2.5 g Sat); 5 mg Cholesterol; 12 g Carbohydrate (1 g Fibre, 1 g Sugar); 3 g Protein; 290 mg Sodium

Sweet and Spicy Pork Casserole

When you're looking for something just a little different, here's a dish to try.
Malt vinegar adds interest to this hearty pork casserole.

All-purpose flour	1/4 cup	60 mL
Granulated sugar	2 tbsp.	30 mL
Boneless pork shoulder butt roast, trimmed of fat and cut into 3/4 inch (2 cm) cubes	4 1/2 lbs.	2 kg
Cooking oil	2 tbsp.	30 mL
Cooking oil	1 tbsp.	15 mL
Thinly sliced onion	2 cups	500 mL
Medium carrots, cut into 1/4 inch (6 mm) slices	3	3
Medium potatoes, peeled and cut into 1/4 inch (6 mm) slices	3	3
Ketchup	1/3 cup	75 mL
Water	1/3 cup	75 mL
Malt vinegar	1/4 cup	60 mL
Worcestershire sauce	3 tbsp.	45 mL

Combine flour and sugar in a large resealable freezer bag. Add pork in 3 batches. Seal bag and toss until pork is coated. Heat first amount of cooking oil in a large frying pan on medium-high. Add pork in several batches. Cook for about 5 minutes per batch, stirring often, until browned on all sides. Transfer to a greased 4 quart (4 L) casserole or medium roasting pan.

Heat second amount of cooking oil in same pan on medium. Add onion cook for 5 to 10 minutes, stirring often, until softened. Add to pork.

Stir in carrot and potato.

Combine remaining 4 ingredients in a small bowl. Stir into pork mixture. Bake, covered, in 350°F (175°C) oven for 2 hours. Stir. Bake, uncovered, for another 20 to 30 minutes until sauce is thickened and pork is tender. Makes 8 servings.

1 serving: 780 Calories; 52 g Total Fat (24 g Mono, 6 g Poly, 17 g Sat); 150 mg Cholesterol; 28 g Carbohydrate (2 g Fibre, 9 g Sugar); 49 g Protein; 310 mg Sodium

Potato Quiche

This cheesy quiche is a perfect weekday meal, but it would also be great as a brunch dish on a lazy, relaxed weekend.

Butter (or margarine)	1 tbsp.	15 mL
Frozen hash brown potatoes	1 1/2 cups	375 mL
Diced ham	1 cup	250 mL
Leeks (white part only), chopped	2	2
Large eggs	3	3
Whipping cream	1 cup	250 mL
Grated Swiss (or Gruyère) cheese	3/4 cup	175 mL
Dried basil	1 tsp.	5 mL
Parsley flakes	3/4 tsp.	4 mL
Salt	3/4 tsp.	4 mL
Pepper	1/4 tsp.	1 mL
Ground nutmeg	1/8 tsp.	0.5 mL
Pastry for 9 inch (23 cm) pie	1	1

Heat butter in a medium frying pan on medium. Add hash browns and leek and cook until browned. Set aside to cool.

Beat eggs in a medium bowl until smooth. Beat in whipping cream. Stir in potato mixture, cheese, basil, parsley, salt, pepper and nutmeg.

Press pastry in bottom and up sides of a springform pan. Pour potato mixture over top. Bake on bottom rack in 350°F (175°C) oven for 45 minutes until knife inserted in centre comes out clean. Cuts into 6 wedges.

*1 **wedge**: 500 Calories; 36 g Total Fat (13 g Mono, 3 g Poly, 17 g Sat); 190 mg Cholesterol; 28 g Carbohydrate (2 g Fibre, 3 g Sugar); 18 g Protein; 1060 mg Sodium*

Dumpling Casserole

Tender sweet potato biscuits on a creamy chicken and ham base. Comfort food at its best! Sprinkle with cinnamon or nutmeg for an attractive presentation.

Cooking oil	1 tbsp.	15 mL
Chopped onion	1 cup	250 mL
Chopped celery	1 cup	250 mL
Sliced fresh mushrooms	1 cup	250 mL
All-purpose flour	1/4 cup	60 mL
Pepper	1/4 tsp.	1 mL
Prepared chicken broth	1 cup	250 mL
Milk	1 1/2 cups	375 mL
Seasoned salt	1/2 tsp.	2 mL
Cooked, cubed chicken	3 cups	750 mL
Cooked, cubed ham	1 cup	250 mL
All-purpose flour	1 1/2 cups	375 mL
Baking powder	1 tbsp.	15 mL
Ground nutmeg	1/4 tsp.	1 mL
Ground cinnamon	1/4 tsp.	1 mL
Salt	1/2 tsp.	2 mL
Large egg, fork-beaten	1	1
Mashed white-fleshed sweet potatoes	2 cups	500 mL
Cooking oil	1/3 cup	75 mL
Milk	1/2 cup	125 mL

Heat cooking oil in a large frying pan on medium-high. Add onion and celery and sauté for about 5 minutes until soft.

Add mushrooms and sauté until soft.

Mix flour and pepper in a small bowl. Gradually whisk in broth until smooth. Add milk and seasoned salt. Stir into onion mixture and cook until boiling and thickened.

Combine chicken and ham in an ungreased 3 quart (3 L) casserole. Add sauce mixture and stir to combine.

For the biscuits, combine next 5 ingredients in a medium bowl.

Beat egg, sweet potato, cooking oil and milk in a small bowl until smooth. Stir into dry ingredients until just moistened. Drop by tablespoonfuls (15 mL) over top of chicken mixture. Bake, uncovered, in 400°F (200°C) oven for 45 minutes until browned. Makes 8 servings.

1 serving: 410 Calories; 17 g Total Fat (9 g Mono, 4 g Poly, 3 g Sat); 50 mg Cholesterol; 36 g Carbohydrate (2 g Fibre, 5 g Sugar); 25 g Protein; 800 mg Sodium

Sausage Vegetable Hash

This hearty casserole is packed with plenty of potatoes, sausage and cheese. Kids and adults alike will love this dish.

Cooking oil	2 tsp.	10 mL
Chopped unpeeled potato	4 cups	1 L
Chopped onion	2 cups	500 mL
Turkey breakfast sausage, sliced	3/4 lb.	340 g
Diced red pepper	1 cup	250 mL
Small cremini mushrooms, whole	1 cup	250 mL
Dried basil	1 tsp.	5 mL
Salt	1/4 tsp.	1 mL
Pepper	1/4 tsp.	1 mL
Garlic clove, minced	1	1
Chopped parsley	1/4 cup	60 mL
Grated mozzarella cheese	1/2 cup	125 mL

Heat cooking oil in a large frying pan on medium. Add next 3 ingredients. Scramble-fry for about 10 minutes until potato starts to soften.

Add next 6 ingredients and cook, stirring, for 3 minutes. Transfer to a greased shallow 2 quart (2 L) casserole. Bake, uncovered, in 400°F (200°C) oven for about 30 minutes until potato is tender.

Stir in parsley. Sprinkle individual servings with cheese. Makes about 7 cups (1.75 L).

1 cup (250 mL): 250 Calories; 15 g Total Fat (1 g Mono, 0 g Poly, 4.5 g Sat); 40 mg Cholesterol; 19 g Carbohydrate (2 g Fibre, 2 g Sugar); 10 g Protein; 340 mg Sodium

Salmon Potato Scallop

Creamy scalloped potatoes sprinkled with salmon. Just add a salad or vegetable, and your dinner is complete.

Medium potatoes, peeled and quartered lengthwise	4	4
Butter (or hard margarine)	1/4 cup	60 mL
Chopped onion	1 cup	250 mL
Chopped green pepper	1/4 cup	60 mL
All-purpose flour	1/4 cup	60 mL
Salt	1 tsp.	5 mL
Pepper	1/4 tsp.	1 mL
Milk	2 cups	500 mL
Cans of red (or pink) salmon (7 1/2 oz., 213 g, each), drained, skin and round bones removed	2	2
Butter (or hard margarine)	2 tbsp.	30 mL
Fine dry bread crumbs	1/2 cup	125 mL
Grated Parmesan cheese	3 tbsp.	45 mL

Cook potato in boiling salted water in a medium saucepan until tender. Drain. Let stand until cool enough to handle. Cut into thin slices. Put 1/2 of potato slices into a greased 2 quart (2 L) casserole. Set aside.

Melt first amount of butter in a medium frying pan on medium. Add onion and green pepper and cook for 5 to 10 minutes, stirring often, until onion is softened.

Add next 3 ingredients. Heat, stirring, for 1 minute.

Slowly add milk, stirring constantly until smooth. Heat, stirring, for 3 to 5 minutes until boiling and thickened. Pour 1/2 of sauce over potato slices in casserole. Scatter salmon over sauce. Layer with remaining potato slices. Pour remaining sauce over top.

Melt second amount of butter in a small saucepan. Remove from heat and add bread crumbs and Parmesan cheese. Stir until well mixed. Sprinkle over sauce. Bake, uncovered, in 350°F (175°C) oven for about 45 minutes until heated through. Makes 6 servings.

1 serving: 390 Calories; 18 g Total Fat (3.5 g Mono, 0.5 g Poly, 10 g Sat); 60 mg Cholesterol; 43 g Carbohydrate (3 g Fibre, 7 g Sugar); 18 g Protein; 850 mg Sodium

Fish Cakes

Fish cakes have been a staple in Newfoundland and Labrador for countless generations. Salt cod was traditionally the fish of choice used for these cakes, and they were often fried in rendered pork fat. In this recipe we've deviated a little from tradition, and the end result is delicious!

Cod fillet	1/2 lb.	225 g
Large egg	1	1
Mashed potatoes	2 cups	500 mL
Soda cracker crumbs	2 tbsp.	30 mL
Lemon juice	1 tsp.	5 mL
Onion powder	1/4 tsp.	1 mL
Parsley flakes	1 tsp.	5 mL
Salt	1/4 tsp.	1 mL
Pepper	1/8 tsp.	0.5 mL
Panko bread crumbs	1/3 cup	75 mL
Butter (or margarine)	2 tbsp.	30 mL

Simmer fish in water in a medium saucepan for about 8 minutes until flaky. Drain. Flake fish in a medium bowl.

Add next 8 ingredients and mix well. Shape into patties using about 1/4 cup (60 mL) for each.

Coat patties with Panko crumbs.

Melt 1 tbsp. (15 mL) butter in a large non-stick frying pan. Brown 4 patties on one side, about 4 to 5 minutes. Turn cakes and fry second side until crispy brown. Transfer to a plate. Repeat with remaining butter and patties. Makes 8 cakes.

1 cake: 110 Calories; 3.5 g Total Fat (1 g Mono, 0 g Poly, 2 g Sat); 20 mg Cholesterol; 12 g Carbohydrate (1 g Fibre, 1 g Sugar); 7 g Protein; 220 mg Sodium

Gnocchi

Soft little pillows of potato dough, gnocchi make a fine base for all kinds of sauces. The finer and fluffier you can mash the cooked potato, the better the texture of the gnocchi will be.

Unpeeled baking potatoes (about 3 medium potatoes)	1 3/4 lb.	790 g
Large eggs, fork-beaten	2	2
Salt	1/2 tsp.	2 mL
Pepper	1/4 tsp.	1 mL
All-purpose flour	1 1/4 cups	300 mL
Grated Parmesan cheese (optional)	1/4 cup	60 mL
All-purpose flour	3 tbsp.	45 mL
Water	8 cups	2 L
Salt	2 tsp.	10 mL

Bake potatoes in 400°F (200°C) oven for about 45 minutes or boil with skin on until tender. Let stand for 10 minutes until cool enough to handle. Remove peel and press potato through a coarse sieve or mash well in a large bowl. Let stand for about 20 minutes until lukewarm. Make a well in centre.

Add next 3 ingredients to well and stir.

Sprinkle flour and cheese over potato mixture. Mix lightly with a fork until mixture starts to come together.

Turn out onto a lightly floured surface. Knead gently 6 times until a ball forms. Divide dough into 6 portions. Keep remaining portions covered. Roll 1 portion into a 3/4 inch (2 cm) thick rope, using second amount of flour as needed to prevent sticking. Cut into 1/2 inch (12 mm) pieces and gently roll tines of a fork along gnocchi to create ridges. Arrange gnocchi in a single layer on a lightly floured baking sheet. Repeat with remaining dough portions.

Combine water and salt in a Dutch oven and bring to a boil. Cook gnocchi, in 2 batches, for about 2 minutes, stirring occasionally, until gnocchi float to the top. Cook for 1 minute before removing with a slotted spoon to a sieve to drain. Transfer to a serving dish. Cover to keep warm. Makes about 4 cups (1 L).

1 cup (250 mL): 340 Calories; 3 g Total Fat (0.5 g Mono, 0.5 g Poly, 1.5 g Sat); 4 mg Cholesterol; 63 g Carbohydrate (5 g Fibre, 1 g Sugar); 13 g Protein; 740 mg Sodium

To store, freeze uncooked gnocchi in a single layer on a lightly floured baking sheet. Store in a resealable freezer bag for up to 3 months. For best results, cook from frozen. Gnocchi can also be pre-cooked, tossed in a little cooking oil or melted butter and chilled. Reheat in boiling water for about 3 minutes. Drain well. Add to your favourite sauce.

Spanish Omelet

In Spain, this dish is served hot or cold, often as an appetizer. Because it is so simple and quick to prepare, we like to serve it as a weekday meal, paired with a garden salad.

Olive (or cooking) oil	1 tbsp.	15 mL
Peeled, cubed potatoes	2 cups	500 mL
Small onion, coarsely chopped	1	1
Large eggs	6	6
Water	3 tbsp.	45 mL
Seasoned salt	1/2 tsp.	2 mL
Pepper	1/4 tsp.	1 mL
Hot pepper sauce	1/4 tsp.	1 mL
Grated Monterey Jack	3/4 cup	175 mL
Chili sauce (or salsa), optional	3 tbsp.	45 mL

Heat olive oil in a non-stick frying pan on medium. Add potato and onion and cook for about 20 minutes until tender. Turn potato several times to brown.

Beat eggs, water, seasoned salt, pepper and hot pepper sauce in a medium bowl. Stir in cheese. Reduce heat under frying pan to low. Pour egg mixture into pan over potatoes. Cook, covered, on low for 8 minutes until bottom is browned.

Drizzle top with chili sauce, if using. Place under broiler (see Tip, below), on top oven rack for 2 minutes until set and golden brown. Cuts into 6 wedges.

1 wedge: 140 Calories; 7 g Total Fat (1.5 g Mono, 0 g Poly, 3 g Sat); 15 mg Cholesterol; 13 g Carbohydrate (1 g Fibre, 3 g Sugar); 8 g Protein; 400 mg Sodium

Tip: When baking or broiling food in a frying pan with a handle that is not ovenproof, wrap the handle in foil and keep it to the front of the oven, away from the element.

Vegetable Shepherd's Pie

This meatless shepherd's pie is packed with so many vegetables and lentils—you won't miss the meat at all!

Large potatoes, peeled and cut up	4	4
Light sour cream	1/3 cup	75 mL
Cooking oil	2 tsp.	10 mL
Medium carrots, thinly sliced	2	2
Medium onion, diced	1	1
Garlic clove, minced (or 1/2 tsp., 2 mL, powder)	2	2
Medium zucchini (with peel), diced	1	1
Sliced fresh white mushrooms	1 cup	250 mL
Can of diced tomatoes (28 oz., 796 mL), drained	1	1
Can of lentils (19 oz., 540 mL), rinsed and drained	1	1
Dried basil	1 tsp.	5 mL
Dried oregano	1 tsp.	5 mL
Salt	1/2 tsp.	2 mL
Onion powder	1/2 tsp.	2 mL
Pepper	1/2 tsp.	2 mL
Ground sage	1/4 tsp.	1 mL
Grated Parmesan cheese	3 tbsp.	45 mL

Cook potato in boiling salted water in a large saucepan until tender. Drain.

Add sour cream and mash. Cover and set aside.

Heat cooking oil in a large saucepan or Dutch oven on medium-high. Add next 3 ingredients and cook for 5 minutes, stirring often.

Add zucchini and mushrooms. Cook for another 4 to 5 minutes, stirring often, until carrot is tender-crisp.

Stir in next 7 ingredients. Reduce heat to medium-low and simmer, uncovered, for about 20 minutes, stirring occasionally, until slightly thickened. Transfer to a greased 3 quart (3 L) casserole.

Spread mashed potatoes on vegetable mixture. Sprinkle with Parmesan cheese. Bake, uncovered, in 350°F (175°C) oven for 30 to 35 minutes until heated through. Broil for about 5 minutes until cheese is golden. Makes 8 servings.

1 serving: 270 Calories; 3.5 g Total Fat (1 g Mono, 0.5 g Poly, 1.5 g Sat); 5 mg Cholesterol; 52 g Carbohydrate (7 g Fibre, 7 g Sugar); 11 g Protein; 600 mg Sodium

Rosti Pizza

Potato and celery root form the crust of this tasty pizza, which is topped with fresh tomatoes and a mild chili heat.

Grated celery root	1 3/4 cups	425 mL
Grated peeled potato	1 3/4 cups	425 mL
Finely chopped onion	1/2 cup	125 mL
Large egg, fork-beaten	1	1
All-purpose flour	1/4 cup	60 mL
Cooking oil	1 tbsp.	15 mL
Dried rosemary, crushed	1/2 tsp.	2 mL
Salt	1/2 tsp.	2 mL
Pepper	1/4 tsp.	1 mL
Cooking oil	2 tbsp.	30 mL
Tomato sauce	1/4 cup	60 mL
Sun-dried tomato pesto	2 tbsp.	30 mL
Dried crushed chilies	1/4 tsp.	1 mL
Grated Italian cheese blend	1 cup	250 mL
Large tomato slices, halved	4	4
Chopped fresh basil	2 tsp.	10 mL

Combine first 3 ingredients in a fine sieve and let stand over a medium bowl for 15 minutes. Squeeze celery root mixture to remove excess moisture. Transfer to a large bowl.

Add next 6 ingredients. Mix well.

Heat 1 tbsp. (15 mL) cooking oil in a large non-stick frying pan on medium. Spoon celery root mixture into pan and press down lightly to cover bottom of pan. Cook for about 10 minutes until bottom is crisp and golden. Slide onto a plate. Heat remaining cooking oil in same frying pan. Invert celery root mixture onto another plate. Slide into pan, golden side up. Cook for about 5 minutes until bottom is crisp and golden.

Combine next 3 ingredients in a small bowl. Spread over celery root mixture, almost to edge. Sprinkle with cheese. Broil on centre rack in oven for about 2 minutes until cheese is melted (see Tip, page 86). Transfer to a cutting board.

Arrange tomato slices over top and sprinkle with basil. Serve immediately. Makes 4 servings.

1 serving: 320 Calories; 15 g Total Fat (4 g Mono, 2 g Poly, 4.5 g Sat); 20 mg Cholesterol; 31 g Carbohydrate (4 g Fibre, 4 g Sugar); 12 g Protein; 400 mg Sodium

Potato Cheese Frittata

This frittata can be done on the stovetop or in the oven. Vary the type of cheese to Swiss, a jalapeño-flavoured Jack cheese or a smoked Cheddar for a terrific flavour change.

Potatoes (about 2 medium), peeled and quartered	1 lb.	454 g
Chopped onion	2/3 cup	150 mL
Cooking oil	1 tsp.	5 mL
Large eggs	3	3
Water	1 tbsp.	15 mL
Parsley flakes	1/4 tsp.	1 mL
Paprika	1/4 tsp.	1 mL
Salt	1/4 tsp.	1 mL
Pepper	1/8 tsp.	0.5 mL
Broccoli florets	1/2 cup	125 mL
Grated light sharp Cheddar cheese	1/2 cup	125 mL

Cook potato in water until tender. Drain and set aside until cool enough to handle. Dice.

Sauté onion in cooking oil in a non-stick frying pan until tender.

Beat next 6 ingredients in a medium bowl until smooth. Stir in potato and broccoli. Pour over onion in pan. Cook, covered, on medium-low for 9 to 10 minutes until almost set.

Sprinkle with cheese. Put pan under broiler near top of oven (see Tip, page 86), until cheese is melted and frittata is set on top. Cuts into 4 wedges.

Oven Method: Sauté onion. Combine all ingredients except cheese in greased 1 quart (1 L) casserole dish. Bake, uncovered, at 350°F (175°C) for 20 minutes. Sprinkle with cheese. Bake or broil for 1 to 2 minutes until cheese is melted.

1 wedge: 170 Calories; 4.5 g Total Fat (0.5 g Mono, 0 g Poly, 2 g Sat); 10 mg Cholesterol; 23 g Carbohydrate (2 g Fibre, 2 g Sugar); 9 g Protein; 310 mg Sodium

Oven Hash Browns

Make this ahead of time and pop it into the oven when you need it. The crunchy topping really sets this dish apart.

Frozen hash browns, thawed	8 cups	1.8 L
Chopped onion	1/2 cup	125 mL
Condensed cream of chicken soup (10 oz., 284 mL)	1	1
Sour cream	2 cups	500 mL
Grated medium Cheddar cheese	2 cups	500 mL
Salt	1 tsp.	5 mL
Pepper	1/4 tsp.	1 mL
Crushed cornflakes	1 cups	250 mL
Panko	1 cup	250 mL
Butter or margarine, melted	1/2 cup	125 mL

Combine first 7 ingredients and pour into a 9 x 13 inch (23 x 33 cm) pan.

In a medium bowl, combine cornflakes and melted butter. Spread over hash brown mixture. Bake, uncovered, in 350°F (180°C) oven for 50 to 60 minutes. Makes 8 servings.

1 serving: 800 Calories; 53 g Total Fat (18 g Mono, 3.5 g Poly, 28 g Sat); 90 mg Cholesterol; 71 g Carbohydrate (4 g Fibre, 5 g Sugar); 16 g Protein; 1040 mg Sodium

Glazed Garlic Potatoes

These golden potatoes are excellent with a roast pork or beef. If you don't have baby new potatoes, use about 6 unpeeled medium new potatoes, cut up.

White (or alcohol-free) wine	1/3 cup	75 mL
Virgin olive oil	3 tbsp.	45 mL
Finely chopped onion	1/3 cup	75 mL
Garlic cloves, finely chopped (not minced)	4	4
Dried rosemary, crushed	1/2 tsp.	2 mL
Dried thyme	1/4 tsp.	1 mL
Salt	1/2 tsp.	2 mL
Freshly ground pepper	1/8 tsp.	0.5 mL
Unpeeled baby potatoes	3 lbs.	1.4 kg

Combine first 8 ingredients in a small saucepan and bring to a boil. Pour into a medium roasting pan.

Add potatoes and stir to coat with spice mixture. Roast, uncovered, in 400°F (200°C) oven for about 60 minutes until tender. Stir and shake potatoes several times while roasting. Makes 8 servings.

1 serving: 200 Calories; 5 g Total Fat (4 g Mono, 0 g Poly, 1 g Sat); 0 mg Cholesterol; 32 g Carbohydrate (2 g Fibre, 0 g Sugar); 4 g Protein; 160 mg Sodium

Colcannon

Colcannon is a traditional Irish dish that dates back to at least the mid-eighteenth century. In its earliest form it may have been little more than a mixture of boiled potatoes and cabbage mashed together, but it has evolved over the years to include leeks or onion, seasonings, butter and in some cases, cream. The traditional way to eat colcannon in Ireland is to heap it into a mountain shape on your plate, then make a depression in the centre and add a pat of butter. The heat of the colcannon melts the butter, and the diner scoops some of the potato/cabbage mixture onto his fork and dips it into the melted butter before eating it. In Ireland the dish is traditionally served on Halloween, which is also known as Colcannon Night.

Peeled potatoes (about 5 medium), cut up	2 1/2 lbs.	1.1 kg
Peeled medium parsnips, cut up	2	2
Medium onions, chopped	2	2
Shredded cabbage, lightly packed	2 cups	500 mL
Butter (or margarine)	1/4 cup	60 mL
Salt	1 tsp.	5 mL
Pepper	1/4 tsp.	1 mL
Green onion, chopped	1/4 cup	60 mL

Boil first 4 ingredients in a large saucepan of water until vegetables are tender. Drain and mash.

Add butter, salt and pepper and mash until butter is melted. Sprinkle with green onion. Makes 6 cups (1.5 L).

1 cup (250 mL): 260 Calories; 8 g Total Fat (2 g Mono, 0 g Poly, 4.5 g Sat); 20 mg Cholesterol; 45 g Carbohydrate (6 g Fibre, 6 g Sugar); 5 g Protein; 460 mg Sodium

Potato Vegetable Kabobs

Fresh lime juice really livens up these grilled veggies. Pair with any grilled meat.

Lime juice	1/4 cup	60 mL
Orange juice	2 tbsp.	30 mL
Sun-dried tomato pesto	2 tbsp.	30 mL
Cooking oil	2 tbsp.	30 mL
White baby potatoes, larger ones cut in half	1 1/2 lbs.	680 g
Large red peppers, cut into 1 1/2 inch (3.8 cm) pieces	2	2
Medium zucchini (with peel), halved lengthwise and cut into 1 inch (2.5 cm) slices	2	2
Bamboo skewers (8 inches, 20 cm, each), soaked in water for 10 minutes	12	12

Combine first 4 ingredients in a small cup. Set aside.

Put potatoes on a microwave-safe plate. Microwave on high (100%) for about 5 minutes until just tender (see Tip, page 12).

Thread potatoes, red pepper and zucchini alternately onto skewers. Place on a large plate. Brush kabobs with half of lime juice mixture. Preheat gas barbecue to medium (see Tip, below). Cook kabobs on a greased grill for about 15 minutes, turning once at halftime and brushing with remaining lime juice mixture, until vegetables are tender-crisp. Makes 6 servings.

1 serving: 180 Calories; 6 g Total Fat (3 g Mono, 1.5 g Poly, 0.5 g Sat); 0 mg Cholesterol; 28 g Carbohydrate (3 g Fibre, 4 g Sugar); 4 g Protein; 45 mg Sodium

Tip: Too cold to barbecue? Use the broiler instead! Your food should cook in about the same length of time—and remember to turn and baste as directed. Set your oven rack so that the food is about 3 to 4 inches (7.5 to 10 cm) away from the top element—for most ovens, this is the top rack.

Gratin Dauphinois

This is quick and easy to put together, and it smells wonderful as it is cooking.

Cooking oil	2 tsp.	10 mL
Garlic clove, halved (optional)	1	1
Potatoes (about 4 medium), peeled and thinly sliced	2 lbs.	900 g
Light cream	1 cup	250 mL
Salt	1/4 tsp.	1 mL
Pepper	1/8 tsp.	0.5 mL
Ground nutmeg	1/8 tsp.	0.5 mL
Grated Gruyère cheese	3/4 cup	175 mL
Grated Gruyère cheese	1/3 cup	75 mL

Rub inside of 2 quart (2 L) casserole with oil and garlic. Layer potato slices in casserole.

Heat cream, salt, pepper, nutmeg and first amount of cheese in a small saucepan until hot. Pour over potato.

Sprinkle with second amount of cheese. Bake, uncovered, in 350°F (175°C) oven for 45 to 50 minutes until potatoes are tender. Makes 6 servings.

1 serving: 250 Calories; 11 g Total Fat (3.5 g Mono, 0.5 g Poly, 7 g Sat); 35 mg Cholesterol; 28 g Carbohydrate (2 g Fibre, 1 g Sugar); 10 g Protein; 190 mg Sodium

Hasselback Potatoes

Turn the humble baked potato into something magnificent! Cut accordion style, these potatoes are the perfect combination of crispy on the outside and velvety smooth on the inside. Add your choice of fresh herbs to the butter for an extra special treat.

Medium potatoes, peeled	6	6
Butter (or margarine), melted	1/4 cup	60 mL
Fine dry bread crumbs	2 tbsp.	30 mL
Finely grated Parmesan cheese	1 tbsp.	15 mL
Salt	1/2 tsp.	2 mL
Coarsely ground pepper	1/8 tsp.	0.5 mL

Place 1 potato on a large spoon. Cut crosswise into 1/4 inch (6 mm) thick slices just to edge of spoon, leaving bottom of potato uncut. Repeat with remaining potatoes. Keep cut potatoes covered with cold water in a bowl. When they are all cut, drain potatoes and pat dry. Arrange, cut side up, in a greased 9 x 13 inch (23 x 33 cm) baking dish.

Brush potatoes with half of butter. Bake, uncovered, in 425°F (220°C) oven for 30 minutes. Brush with remaining butter. Bake for 15 minutes.

Combine remaining 4 ingredients in a small dish. Sprinkle evenly over potatoes. Bake for 15 minutes until tender and crumbs are golden brown. Makes 6 servings.

1 serving: 240 Calories; 8 g Total Fat (2 g Mono, 0 g Poly, 5 g Sat); 20 mg Cholesterol; 39 g Carbohydrate (4 g Fibre, 2 g Sugar); 5 g Protein; 290 mg Sodium

Duchess Potatoes

Lots of variations make this recipe very versatile for a buffet or individual servings. Brush the top with cooking oil for crispier crust, if desired.

Peeled, quartered potatoes (about 4 medium)	2 lbs.	900 g
Butter (or margarine), softened	2 tbsp.	30 mL
Large eggs, fork-beaten	2	2
Seasoned salt	1/4 tsp.	1 mL
Onion powder	1/8 tsp.	0.5 mL
Pepper (white is best)	1/8 tsp.	0.5 mL
Milk	1/4 cup	60 mL

Cook potato in water in a large saucepan until tender. Drain and mash.

Mix next 6 ingredients in a large bowl. Mix in potato. Using a large star tip in a piping bag, form into 12 swirls on a greased baking sheet or spoon about 1/3 cup (75 mL) into mounds. Spike or dimple with spoon or knife.

Bake in 425°F (220°C) oven for about 20 minutes until tips are golden. Makes 12 mounds.

1 mound: 80 Calories; 2 g Total Fat (0 g Mono, 0 g Poly, 1.5 g Sat); 5 mg Cholesterol; 14 g Carbohydrate (1 g Fibre, 1 g Sugar); 2 g Protein; 60 mg Sodium

Duchess Cheese Potatoes: Add 1 cup (250 mL) grated medium or sharp Cheddar cheese with margarine, eggs, seasonings and milk.

Duchess Potato Casserole: Double or triple recipe. Pack 1/2 into greased 2 or 3 quart (2 or 3 L) casserole. Pipe remaining 1/2 into swirls all over top. Bake in 350°F (175°C) oven for 25 to 30 minutes until hot.

Parmesan Duchess Potatoes: Add 2 tbsp. (30 mL) grated Parmesan cheese with margarine, eggs, seasonings and milk.

Mixed Duchess Potatoes: Omit milk. Add 1/4 cup (60 mL) sour cream and 2 tbsp. (30 mL) chopped chives.

Crunchy Potato Balls

These potato balls have way more flavour and way less fat than frozen potato puffs. Adults won't be able to resist them either! Serve with hot dogs or hamburgers.

Peeled potatoes, cut up (about 2 medium)	1 lb.	454 g
Large egg, fork-beaten	1	1
Grated Swiss cheese	1/2 cup	125 mL
Mayonnaise	2 tbsp.	30 mL
Finely chopped green onion	1 tbsp.	15 mL
Fine dry bread crumbs	3/4 cup	175 mL
Seasoned salt	1/2 tsp.	2 mL
Cooking oil	2 tsp.	10 mL

Cook potato in water in a medium saucepan until tender. Drain and mash. Let stand until cool enough to handle.

Combine next 4 ingredients in a large bowl. Add potato, stirring well. Roll into 1 inch (2.5 cm) balls.

Combine bread crumbs and seasoned salt in a large shallow dish. Press and roll balls in crumb mixture until coated. Arrange on a greased baking sheet with sides.

Brush with cooking oil. Bake in 350°F (175°C) oven for about 30 minutes until golden. Makes 4 servings.

1 serving: 280 Calories; 10 g Total Fat (4 g Mono, 1.5 g Poly, 3 g Sat); 15 mg Cholesterol; 38 g Carbohydrate (2 g Fibre, 2 g Sugar); 10 g Protein; 530 mg Sodium

Spicy Potato Bumps

Think of these as dressed up, spicy, oven-baked hash browns. Use your favourite combination of spices these, and they would still be as delicious!

Unpeeled medium baking potatoes	6	6
Olive oil	1 tbsp.	15 mL
Parsley flakes	2 tsp.	10 mL
Salt	1 1/2 tsp.	7 mL
Chili powder	1 tsp.	5 mL
Paprika	1 tsp.	5 mL
Dried thyme, crushed	1/2 tsp.	2 mL
Garlic powder	1/4 tsp.	1 mL
Cayenne pepper	1/8 tsp.	0.5 mL
Ground rosemary	1/8 tsp.	0.5 mL

Cut each potato in quarters lengthwise. Cut each quarter crosswise into 3 pieces. Toss potato with olive oil in a large bowl.

Combine remaining 8 ingredients in a small cup. Sprinkle over potato and toss to coat. Spread on a large greased baking sheet with sides. Bake, uncovered, in centre of 425°F (220°C) oven. Cook for about 45 minutes, stirring twice, until browned and tender. Makes 6 servings.

1 serving: 190 Calories; 2.5 g Total Fat (1.5 g Mono, 0 g Poly, 0 g Sat); 0 mg Cholesterol; 38 g Carbohydrate (4 g Fibre, 2 g Sugar); 4 g Protein; 600 mg Sodium

Smashed Curried Potatoes

Those of you who prefer a little texture in your mashed potatoes will really appreciate this dish. Smashed potatoes combine the creamy goodness of mashed potatoes with a crispy outer shell. The warm curry spices add even more flair to this delicious side.

Multicoloured baby potatoes	1 lb.	454 g
Small onion, halved	1	1
Curry powder	1 tsp.	5 mL
Butter, melted	2 tbsp.	30 mL
Garam masala	1/2 tsp.	2 mL
Ground coriander	1/2 tsp.	2 mL
Ground cumin	1/2 tsp.	2 mL
Salt	1/8 tsp.	0.5 mL
Garam masala	1/4 tsp.	1 mL

Cook first 3 ingredients in a large saucepan of boiling salted water on medium for 20 minutes until potatoes are tender. Drain and discard onion. Arrange potatoes in a single layer on a greased baking sheet. Press potatoes with bottom of a cup or bowl until flattened.

Combine next 5 ingredients and brush over potatoes. Broil on top rack in oven for 10 minutes until browned and crisp.

Sprinkle with garam masala. Makes about 20 smashed potatoes.

1 smashed potato: 30 Calories; 1 g Total Fat (0 g Mono, 0 g Poly, 0.5 g Sat); 0 mg Cholesterol; 4 g Carbohydrate (0 g Fibre, 0 g Sugar); 1 g Protein; 25 mg Sodium

Grilled Potato Wedges

These crispy-crumbed wedges have a great smoky flavour that pairs perfectly with steaks or burgers. If you'd prefer not to grill them, you can bake them, skin-side down, on a greased baking sheet with sides in a 450°F (230°C) oven for about 30 minutes until tender.

All-purpose flour	1/2 cup	125 mL
Fine dry bread crumbs	1/2 cup	125 mL
Garlic powder	1 tsp.	5 mL
Seasoned salt	1 tsp.	5 mL
Pepper	1/2 tsp.	2 mL
Large eggs	2	2
Medium unpeeled baking potatoes, cut lengthwise into 1/2 inch (12 mm) wedges	4	4
Cooking spray		

Combine first 5 ingredients in a large resealable freezer bag.

Whisk eggs in a large bowl. Add potato and toss until coated. Transfer half of potato to flour mixture. Toss until coated. Shake off excess flour mixture. Place, skin-side down, on a large baking sheet. Repeat with remaining potato.

Spray potato with cooking spray. Preheat your gas barbecue to medium. Arrange wedges on their sides on a greased grill. Close lid. Cook for about 12 minutes per side until browned and tender. Makes 8 servings.

1 serving: 140 Calories; 0 g Total Fat (0 g Mono, 0 g Poly, 0 g Sat); 0 mg Cholesterol; 31 g Carbohydrate (2 g Fibre, 1 g Sugar); 5 g Protein; 290 mg Sodium

Mushroom Cheese Braids

Almost too pretty to be a side dish! You could serve it as a first course or appetizer as well.

Mashed potatoes	2 cups	500 mL
Large egg	1	1
Salt	1/2 tsp.	2 mL
Pepper	1/4 tsp.	1 mL
Grated Parmesan cheese	2 tbsp.	30 mL
All-purpose flour	1 1/4 cups	300 mL
Butter (or margarine)	1 tbsp.	15 mL
Sliced fresh mushrooms	1 1/2 cups	375 mL
Chopped green onion	1/4 cup	60 mL
Grated Gruyère cheese	1 cup	250 mL
Parsley flakes	1 tsp.	5 mL
Garlic powder (optional)	1/4 tsp.	1 mL
Large egg, fork-beaten	1	1
Grated Parmesan cheese, to taste		

For the crust, mix first 6 ingredients in a medium bowl to make a soft dough. Roll out 1/2 on a well-floured surface into 12 x 9 inch (30 x 23 cm) rectangle.

For the filling, melt butter in a medium frying pan on medium-high. Add mushrooms and sauté until golden. Transfer to a medium bowl and set aside to cool slightly.

Stir in next 4 ingredients. Spoon 1/2 of filling down length in centre third of rectangle. Cut perpendicular slits in dough about 1 inch (2.5 cm) wide from filling outward to edges. Fold strips to cross over centre portion in a braid design. Repeat with second 1/2 of pastry and filling.

Carefully transfer braids to a greased baking sheet using a pancake lifter. Brush tops with egg and sprinkle with Parmesan cheese. Bake in 375°F (190°C) oven for 25 to 30 minutes until golden brown. Cuts into 12 slices.

1 slice: 130 Calories; 4.5 g Total Fat (1.5 g Mono, 0 g Poly, 2.5 g Sat); 15 mg Cholesterol; 16 g Carbohydrate (1 g Fibre, 1 g Sugar); 6 g Protein; 170 mg Sodium

Coconut Potatoes

In Thailand this would be made with several cloves of garlic, so feel free to adjust the number of cloves to suit your tastes.

Peeled potatoes (about 3 medium), cut into 1/4 inch (6 mm) thick slices	1 1/2 lbs.	680 g
Cooking oil	2 tsp.	10 mL
Garlic clove, minced	1	1
Can of coconut milk (14 oz. 400 mL)	1	1
All-purpose flour	1/3 cup	75 mL
Salt	1/2 tsp.	2 mL
Pepper	1/8 tsp.	0.5 mL
Water	1/2 cup	125 mL
Toasted sesame seeds, optional	2 tbsp.	30 mL

Cook potato in a large saucepan of boiling salted water on medium until tender. Drain.

Heat cooking oil in a frying pan on medium-high. Add garlic and sauté until golden.

Add coconut milk and cook, stirring, until hot.

Combine flour, salt and pepper in a small bowl. Gradually whisk in water until smooth. Stir into milk mixture until boiling and thickened. Stir in potato and turn into an ungreased 2 quart (2 L) casserole. Bake in 350°F (175°C) oven for 20 minutes.

Sprinkle with sesame seeds. Bake for 10 to 15 minutes until golden brown. Makes 4 servings.

1 serving: 410 Calories; 26 g Total Fat (3.5 g Mono, 2 g Poly, 19 g Sat); 0 mg Cholesterol; 41 g Carbohydrate (3 g Fibre, 1 g Sugar); 8 g Protein; 320 mg Sodium

Latkes

Latkes are a type of Jewish fried pancake that is traditionally served at Hanukkah. Although latkes can be made from many types of vegetables, such as sweet potato, cabbage or parsnips, potato latkes are the most common variety. The secret to the perfect potato latke is to remove as much moisture as possible from the shredded potato before mixing in the remaining ingredients

Peeled, grated potatoes	4 cups	1 L
Medium onion, grated	1	1
Large eggs, fork-beaten	2	2
All-purpose flour	1/2 cup	125 mL
Salt	1 1/2 tsp.	7 mL
Pepper	1/4 tsp.	1 mL
Cooking oil	1 cup	250 mL

Squeeze excess water from grated potato and drain well. Place in a large bowl.

Add next 5 ingredients and stir well.

Heat cooking oil in a large cast-iron or heavy frying pan. Drop potato mixture by 1/4 cupfuls (60 mL) into pan. Flatten to 3 to 4 inch (7 to 10 cm) patty. Fry for about 3 minutes per side until golden brown and crispy. Drain on paper towels. Makes 12 latkes.

1 latke: 110 Calories; 4.5 g Total Fat (3 g Mono, 1 g Poly, 0 g Sat); 0 mg Cholesterol; 14 g Carbohydrate (1 g Fibre, 1 g Sugar); 2 g Protein; 300 mg Sodium

Bacon and Cheese Spuds

This side is hearty enough to be served as a main, as well. Just pair it with a garden salad for a complete meal.

Medium potatoes, baked	4	4
Herb-flavored non-fat spreadable cream cheese	1/4 cup	60 mL
Milk	1 tbsp.	15 mL
Grated light sharp Cheddar cheese	1/4 cup	60 mL
Salt	1/4 tsp.	1 mL
Pepper	1/8 tsp.	0.5 mL
Bacon slices, diced	3	3
Chopped fresh mushrooms	1/2 cup	125 mL
Chopped green onion	2 tbsp.	30 mL
Grated light sharp Cheddar cheese	1/4 cup	60 mL

Cut 1/4 inch (6 mm) lengthwise from top of each potato. Scoop out pulp into a medium bowl, leaving shells 1/4 inch (6 mm) thick. Discard tops once pulp is removed. Mash pulp.

Add next 5 ingredients and beat until smooth.

Cook bacon in a frying pan on medium for 3 to 4 minutes until crisp. Remove bacon with a slotted spoon and add to potato pulp, reserving about 1 tbsp. (15 mL) for garnish.

Drain all but 1 tsp. (5 mL) fat from frying pan. Add mushrooms and green onion and cook until soft. Stir into potato pulp and stuff mixture into potato shells.

Arrange on an ungreased baking sheet. Sprinkle with second amount of Cheddar cheese and reserved bacon. Bake in 350°F (175°C) oven for 20 minutes until heated through. Makes 4 stuffed potatoes.

1 stuffed potato: 350 Calories; 19 g Total Fat (6 g Mono, 1.5 g Poly, 8 g Sat); 40 mg Cholesterol; 39 g Carbohydrate (4 g Fibre, 3 g Sugar); 12 g Protein; 560 mg Sodium

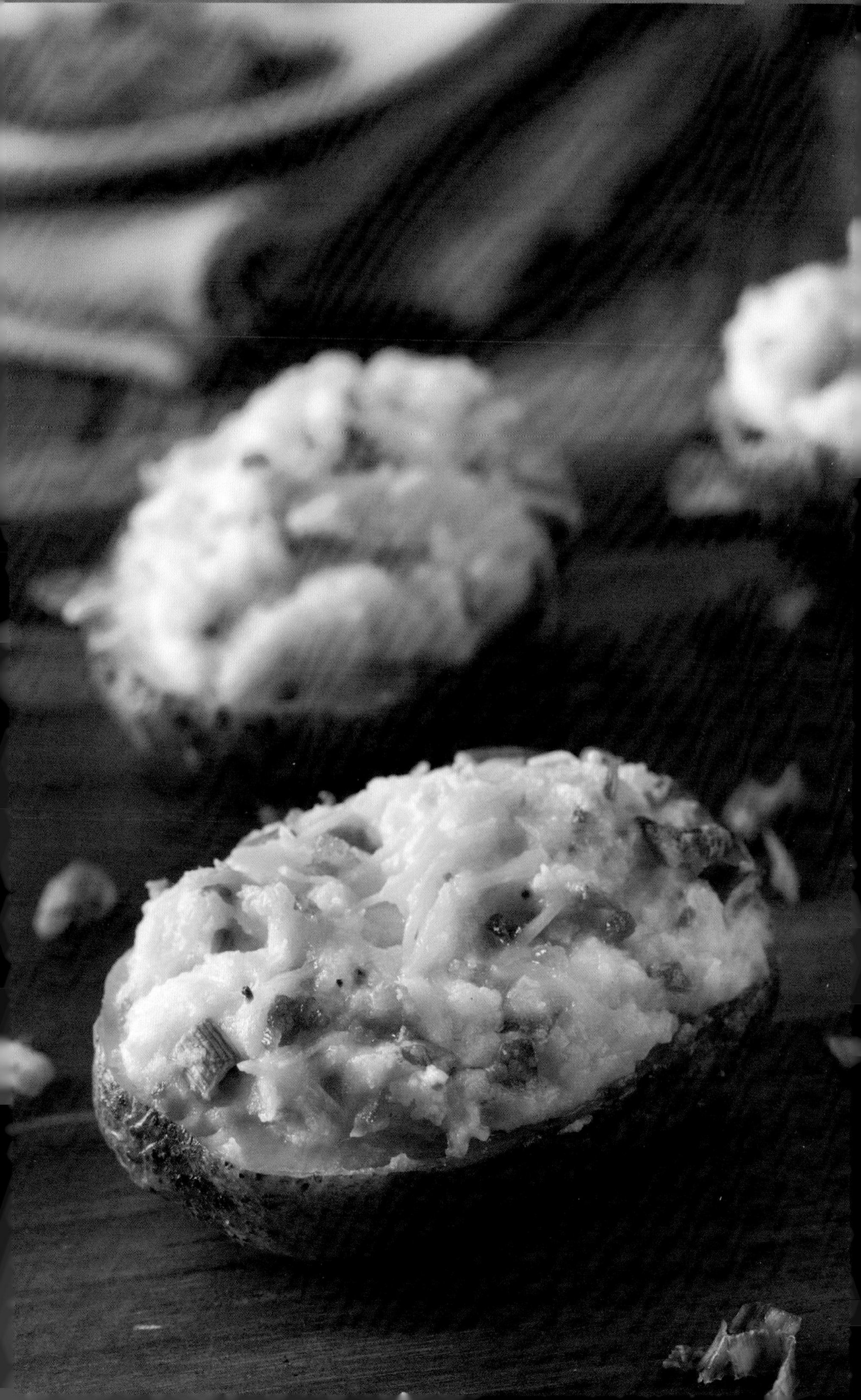

Perogies

These tender perogies are filled with potato, onion and Cheddar cheese. Feel free to change up the filling and add your favourites ingredeints; bacon, roasted garlic or cottage cheese would also be delicous in the mix! Garnish with fresh herbs, such as parsley or dill for an attractive presentation.

All-purpose flour	2 cups	500 mL
Salt	1/2 tsp.	2 mL
Mashed baking potatoes (see Note)	1 1/2 cups	375 mL
Large egg, fork-beaten	1	1
Warm water (if needed)	1/4 cup	60 mL
Mashed potatoes	3 cups	750 mL
Grated sharp Cheddar cheese	1 1/3 cups	325 mL
Finely chopped onion	3 tbsp.	45 mL
Butter (or margarine), melted	3 tbsp.	45 mL
Salt	3/4 tsp.	4 mL
White pepper	1/8 tsp.	0.5 mL
Water	4 qts.	4 L
Salt	1 tbsp.	15 mL
Butter (or margarine), melted (optional)		

For the dough, combine flour and salt in a large bowl. Make a well. Stir in mashed potato and egg. Add enough warm water to make a soft dough that can be rolled. Cover with plastic wrap and let rest for 20 minutes.

For the filling, combine next 6 ingredients in a medium bowl. Roll 1/3 of dough to a 12 inch (30 cm) circle on a well-floured surface. Cover remaining dough to prevent it from drying out. Cut 3 inch (7 cm) rounds. Fill each with 1 tbsp. (15 mL) filling. Dampen edge and fold dough over, presssing edges together tightly to seal. Arrange on a floured cloth on a flat surface. Cover with a cloth to prevent dough from drying out. Repeat, re-rolling scraps of dough, until dough and filling are used up.

Combine water and salt in a large pot. Add perogies in batches and cook, stirring frequently, for 2 minutes until they rise to surface of water and bob for about 1 minute. Remove with a slotted spoon to a bowl. To prevent sticking, lightly coat with melted butter, if desired. Makes about 54 perogies.

6 perogies: 270 Calories; 9 g Total Fat (2.5 g Mono, 0 g Poly, 6 g Sat); 25 mg Cholesterol; 38 g Carbohydrate (2 g Fibre, 1 g Sugar); 9 g Protein; 590 mg Sodium

Note: Baking potatoes are best for the crust because of their dry texture. They can be used for the filling as well.

To make ahead, lay the cooked perogies in single layer on a greased baking sheet and place it in the freezer until the perogies are hard. Transfer the frozen perogies to a freezer plastic bag to store.

Golden Asiago Potatoes

This layered potato dish is filled with the rich flavours of Asiago and rosemary. Serve with roasted chicken, baked ham or roast beef.

Grated Asiago cheese	1/2 cup	125 mL
Garlic butter, melted	2 tbsp.	30 mL
Chopped fresh rosemary	1 tsp.	5 mL
(or 1/4 tsp., 1 mL, dried, crushed)		
Thinly sliced peeled potato	5 cups	1.25 L
Garlic butter, melted	1 tbsp.	15 mL

Combine first 3 ingredients in a large bowl.

Add potato and toss until coated. Brush bottom and sides of 9 inch (23 cm) pie plate with second amount of melted garlic butter. Arrange potato in overlapping layers. Bake in 425°F (220°C) oven for about 40 minutes until tender. Run knife around inside edge of pie plate to loosen potato. Invert onto a large plate. Cuts into 8 wedges.

1 wedge: 140 Calories; 6 g Total Fat (1.5 g Mono, 0 g Poly, 4 g Sat); 15 mg Cholesterol; 17 g Carbohydrate (1 g Fibre, 1 g Sugar); 4 g Protein; 130 mg Sodium

Sweet Potato Bake

This dish is so yummy it tastes like dessert instead of a side. The sweetness of the brown sugar is somewhat tempered by the subtle orange overtones.

Cooked sweet potatoes, coarsely mashed	3 cups	750 mL
Large eggs	2	2
Grated orange peel	1 1/2 tsp.	7 mL
Freshly squeezed orange juice	3 tbsp.	45 mL
Granulated sugar	2 tbsp.	30 mL
Vanilla extract	1 tsp.	5 mL
Salt	1/4 tsp.	1 mL
Butter (or margarine)	3 tbsp.	45 mL
Brown sugar, packed	1/2 cup	125 mL
All-purpose flour	1/4 cup	60 mL

Stir first 7 ingredients in a medium bowl. Turn into an ungreased shallow 2 quart (2 L) casserole.

Melt butter in a small saucepan. Stir in brown sugar and flour. Sprinkle over sweet potato mixture. Bake, uncovered, in 350°F (175°C) oven for 45 minutes until hot and set. Makes 6 servings.

1 serving: 240 Calories; 6 g Total Fat (1.5 g Mono, 0 g Poly, 3.5 g Sat); 15 mg Cholesterol; 40 g Carbohydrate (2 g Fibre, 25 g Sugar); 3 g Protein; 200 mg Sodium

Heaven and Earth

How can you not love that delicious bacon and onion flavor?! To dress up this German dish, garnish with red apple slices and bacon.

Peeled, cubed potatoes (about 4 medium)	2 lbs.	900 g
Peeled, sliced medium cooking apples (such as McIntosh)	5	5
Bacon slices, diced	8	8
Medium onion, chopped	1	1

Cook potato in salted water in a large saucepan until tender-crisp.

Add apple and cook until both apple and potato are tender. Drain and keep hot.

Cook bacon in a medium frying pan on medium for about 4 minutes until starting to brown.

Add onion. Cook, stirring occasionally, until bacon and onion are browned. Drain well. Coarsely mash potato and apple. Stir in 3/4 of bacon-onion mixture. Turn into serving bowl. Sprinkle with remaining bacon and onion. Makes 5 cups (1.25 L).

1 cup (250 mL): 470 Calories; 28 g Total Fat (12 g Mono, 3 g Poly, 9 g Sat); 40 mg Cholesterol; 46 g Carbohydrate (4 g Fibre, 11 g Sugar); 11 g Protein; 520 mg Sodium

Potato Croquettes

These croquettes are creamy and rich inside, with a thick golden crust. A very special treat! They freeze well, so you can keep a stock on hand in the freezer and pull them out when you need them.

Peeled potatoes (about 2 medium), cut up	1 lb.	454 g
Butter (or margarine)	3 tbsp.	45 mL
Finely chopped onion	1/4 cup	60 mL
Finely chopped celery	1/4 cup	60 mL
All-purpose flour	7 tbsp.	110 mL
Whole milk	1 cup	250 mL
Salt	3/4 tsp.	4 mL
Pepper	1/8 tsp.	0.5 mL
Dill weed	1/2 tsp.	2 mL
Ground nutmeg, to taste		
Large eggs	2	2
Cold water	2 tbsp.	30 mL
Fine dry bread crumbs	1 1/3 cups	325 mL
Cooking oil, for deep-frying		

Cook potato in salted water in a medium saucepan until tender. Drain and return to heat. Gently shake to dry. Break potato into small pieces with a fork, or coarsely mash.

Melt butter in a large saucepan over medium. Add onion and celery and cook until very soft. Stir in flour. Slowly add milk, stirring constantly, until sauce is smooth. Heat, stirring, until boiling and thickened.

Stir in salt, pepper, dill and nutmeg. Mixture will be like a thick glue or paste. Stir in potatoes and spread mixture out evenly in a 9 inch (23 cm) pie plate. Lay plastic wrap directly on surface and chill for several hours or overnight (or put into freezer for 1 hour until very cold, but not frozen). Divide into 8 wedges with a knife or shape into 8 patties.

Beat eggs and water with a fork in a shallow dish.

Pour crumbs into a separate shallow dish. Carefully place potato wedge into bread crumbs and form wedge into a cylinder shape. Coat completely. Roll gently in egg mixture and coat in crumbs again. Repeat for total of 2 egg and 3 crumb coats. Chill on waxed paper for 1/2 hour to dry.

Deep-fry in 375°F (190°C) cooking oil for 2 1/2 to 3 minutes, turning gently once or twice, until golden. Remove with a slotted spoon to paper towels to drain. Makes 8 croquettes.

1 croquette: 300 Calories; 10 g Total Fat (3 g Mono, 1 g Poly, 4 g Sat); 15 mg Cholesterol; 48 g Carbohydrate (3 g Fibre, 4 g Sugar); 9 g Protein; 730 mg Sodium

To make ahead, cool the croquettes after they have been deep-fried. Wrap, label and freeze them. Reheat them from a frozen state, on baking sheet in 350°F (175°C) oven for 30 minutes.

Creamy Roasted Garlic Potatoes

A delicious mashed potato casserole designed to be made ahead—one less thing to worry about before a big dinner. This can be made in the morning and reheated later, or prepared and frozen up to a month in advance.

Garlic bulbs	2	2
Cooking oil	1 tbsp.	15 mL
Peeled potatoes, cut up	3 lbs.	1.4 kg
Half-and-half cream	2/3 cup	150 mL
Butter (or hard margarine)	3 tbsp.	45 mL
Finely chopped green onion	3 tbsp.	45 mL
Salt	1 tsp.	5 mL
Pepper	1/4 tsp.	1 mL
Grated havarti cheese	1 cup	250 mL
Coarsely ground pepper, for garnish		

Trim 1/4 inch (6 mm) from garlic bulbs to expose tops of cloves, leaving bulbs intact. Drizzle with cooking oil. Wrap loosely in greased foil. Cook in 375°F (190°C) oven for about 45 minutes until tender. Let stand until cool enough to handle. Squeeze garlic bulbs to remove cloves from skin. Discard skin. Mash garlic with a fork on a small plate until smooth.

Pour water into a large saucepan until 1 inch (2.5 cm) deep. Add potato, cover with lid and bring to a boil. Reduce heat to medium and boil gently for 12 to 15 minutes until tender. Drain well and mash.

Add next 5 ingredients and garlic. Mash.

Stir in cheese and spread evenly in a well-greased 2 quart (2 L) casserole. Sprinkle with pepper. Store in an airtight container in refrigerator for up to 2 days or in freezer for up to 1 month. Thaw in refrigerator before cooking. Cook, covered, in 350°F (175°C) oven for about 1 1/2 hours until internal temperature reaches 165°F (74°C).

Makes about 8 1/2 cups (2.1 L).

1 cup (250 mL): 260 Calories; 12 g Total Fat (3 g Mono, 0.5 g Poly, 6 g Sat); 35 mg Cholesterol; 31 g Carbohydrate (3 g Fibre, 2 g Sugar); 7 g Protein; 410 mg Sodium

Creamy Spinach Potatoes

A delicious way to add spinach to your diet. Decorate with fresh spinach leaves and lemon zest if desired.

Peeled potatoes (about 3 medium), cut up	1 1/2 lbs.	680 g
Butter (or margarine)	2 tbsp.	30 mL
All-purpose flour	1/4 cup	60 mL
Milk	2 cups	500 mL
Onion salt	1/2 tsp.	2 mL
Salt	1/2 tsp.	2 mL
Pepper	1/8 tsp.	0.5 mL
Garlic powder (optional)	1/4 tsp.	1 mL
Package of frozen chopped spinach (10 oz., 300 g), thawed and squeezed dry	1	1
Grated Parmesan cheese	1 tbsp.	15 mL

Cook potato in salted water in a medium saucepan until tender. Drain and coarsely mash.

Melt butter in a medium saucepan. Stir in flour until smooth. Slowly whisk in milk. Add next 4 ingredients and cook, stirring, until boiling and thickened.

Stir in spinach. Turn potato into a greased 2 quart (2 L) baking dish and pour sauce over top. Poke randomly with a spoon to allow some sauce down into potato. Sprinkle with Parmesan cheese. Bake in 350°F (175°C) oven for 30 minutes until hot. Makes 6 servings.

1 serving: 230 Calories; 6 g Total Fat (1 g Mono, 0 g Poly, 3.5 g Sat); 20 mg Cholesterol; 35 g Carbohydrate (10 g Fibre, 3 g Sugar); 12 g Protein; 610 mg Sodium

Double Cheese Potatoes

The cream cheese, sour cream and Cheddar make these potatoes rich and decadent. They pair perfectly with any roasted meat. They are also another great make-ahead option.

Peeled potatoes (about 8 medium), cut up	4 lbs.	1.8 kg
Light cream cheese, softened	8 oz.	250 g
Light sour cream	1 cup	250 mL
Milk	1/2 cup	125 mL
Onion salt	1 tbsp.	15 mL
Pepper	1/4 tsp.	1 mL
Grated sharp white Cheddar cheese	3/4 cup	175 mL
Paprika, as a garnish		

Cook potato in water in a large uncovered pot or Dutch oven until tender. Drain and mash.

Beat cream cheese and sour cream in a medium microwave-safe bowl until smooth. Add milk, onion salt and pepper. Beat well. Heat in microwave on high (100%) until hot (see Tip, page 12). Add to potato and mash well.

Stir in Cheddar cheese. Sprinkle with paprika. Makes 8 cups (2 L).

1 cup (250 mL): 290 Calories; 8 g Total Fat (2 g Mono, 0 g Poly, 4.5 g Sat); 25 mg Cholesterol; 45 g Carbohydrate (3 g Fibre, 3 g Sugar); 13 g Protein; 910 mg Sodium

To make ahead, spread potato mixture in a 3 quart (3 L) covered casserole and chill for up to 2 days. Do not freeze. Bake, covered, in 350°F (175°C) oven for about 1 hour until it is warmed through.

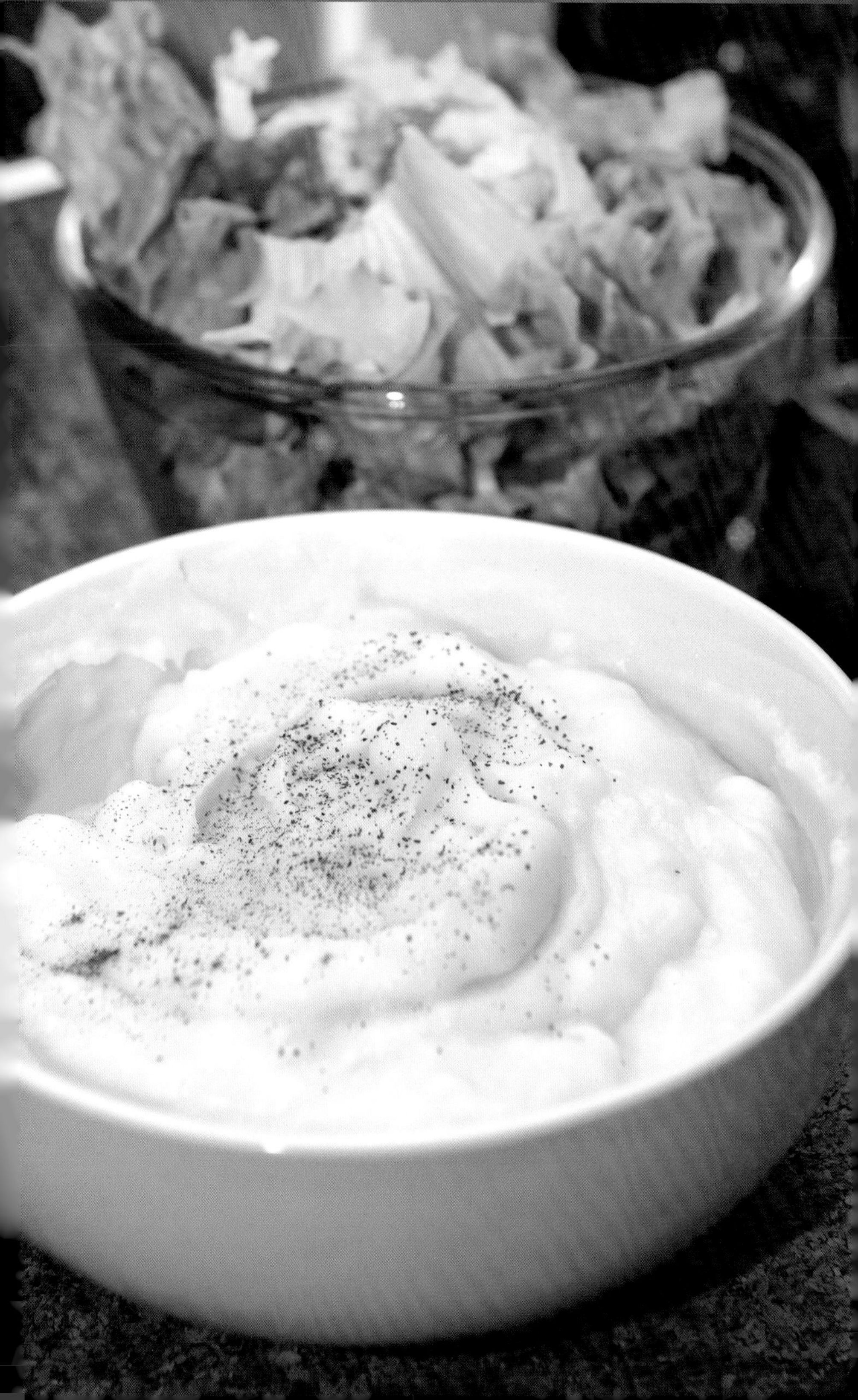

Potato and Celery Root Purée

A unique stand-in for the usual mashed potatoes. This simple recipe allows celery root's delicate flavour to come through in a light and creamy purée.

Chopped celery root	7 cups	1.75 L
Chopped peeled potato	3 cups	750 mL
Milk	1/2 cup	125 mL
Butter (or hard margarine)	1/4 cup	60 mL
Salt	1/2 tsp.	2 mL
White pepper (or black), to taste		

Pour water into a Dutch oven until about 1 inch (2.5 cm) deep. Add celery root and potato and bring to a boil. Reduce heat to medium and boil gently, covered, for 12 to 15 minutes until tender. Drain and cover to keep warm.

Combine remaining 4 ingredients in a small saucepan and bring to a boil. Stir into celery root mixture. Carefully process in a food processor in batches until smooth, following manufacturer's instructions for processing hot liquids. Makes about 6 1/2 cups (1.6 L).

1 cup (250 mL): 180 Calories; 7 g Total Fat (2 g Mono, 0 g Poly, 4.5 g Sat); 20 mg Cholesterol; 25 g Carbohydrate (4 g Fibre, 4 g Sugar); 4 g Protein; 370 mg Sodium

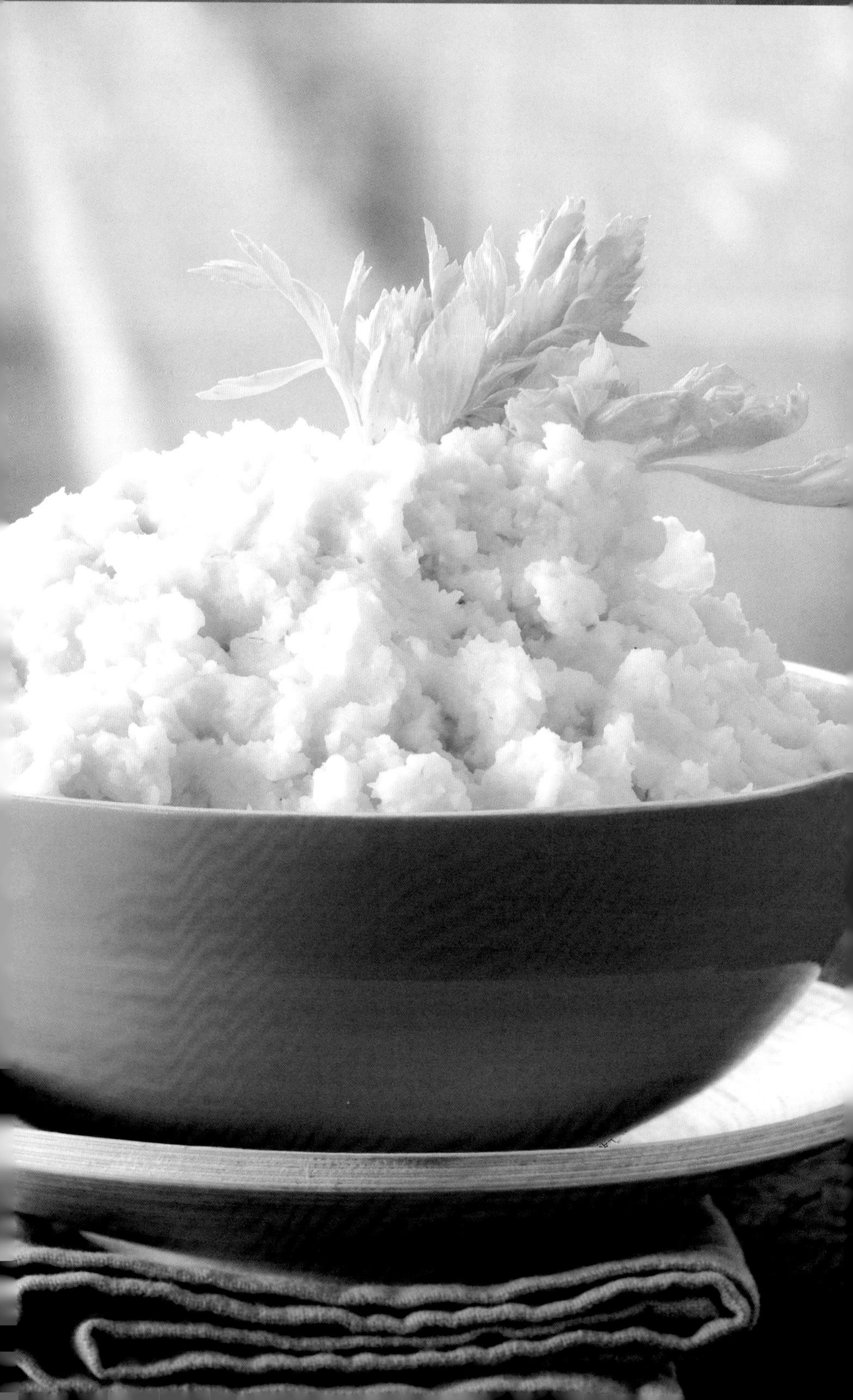

Potato Soufflé

Most soufflés won't wait. This one sits in the oven and stays fluffy until ready to serve.

Butter (or margarine), softened	1 tbsp.	15 mL
Grated Parmesan cheese	1/2 cup	125 mL
Hot mashed potatoes	2 cups	500 mL
Hot milk	1/2 cup	125 mL
Butter (or margarine)	2 tsp.	10 mL
Chopped fresh rosemary (or 1 1/2 tsp., 7 mL, dried)	2 tbsp.	30 mL
Salt	1/2 tsp.	2 mL
Pepper	1/4 tsp.	1 mL
Egg yolks (large)	3	3
Reserved Parmesan cheese		
Egg whites (large), room temperature	3	3
Cream of tartar	1/2 tsp.	2 mL

Grease sides and bottom of soufflé dish or 1 quart (1 L) casserole well with butter. Coat well with Parmesan cheese. Empty excess cheese into a small dish and set aside.

Beat next 8 ingredients in a large bowl on low until fluffy.

Beat egg whites with clean beaters in a medium bowl until peaks are stiff but not dry. Fold 1/3 of egg whites into potato mixture just until mixed. Fold in remaining egg whites. Turn into prepared soufflé dish. Bake on bottom rack of 350°F (175°C) oven for 35 minutes. Makes 6 servings.

1 serving: 150 Calories; 7 g Total Fat (2 g Mono, 0.5 g Poly, 3.5 g Sat); 120 mg Cholesterol; 13 g Carbohydrate (1 g Fibre, 2 g Sugar); 9 g Protein; 390 mg Sodium

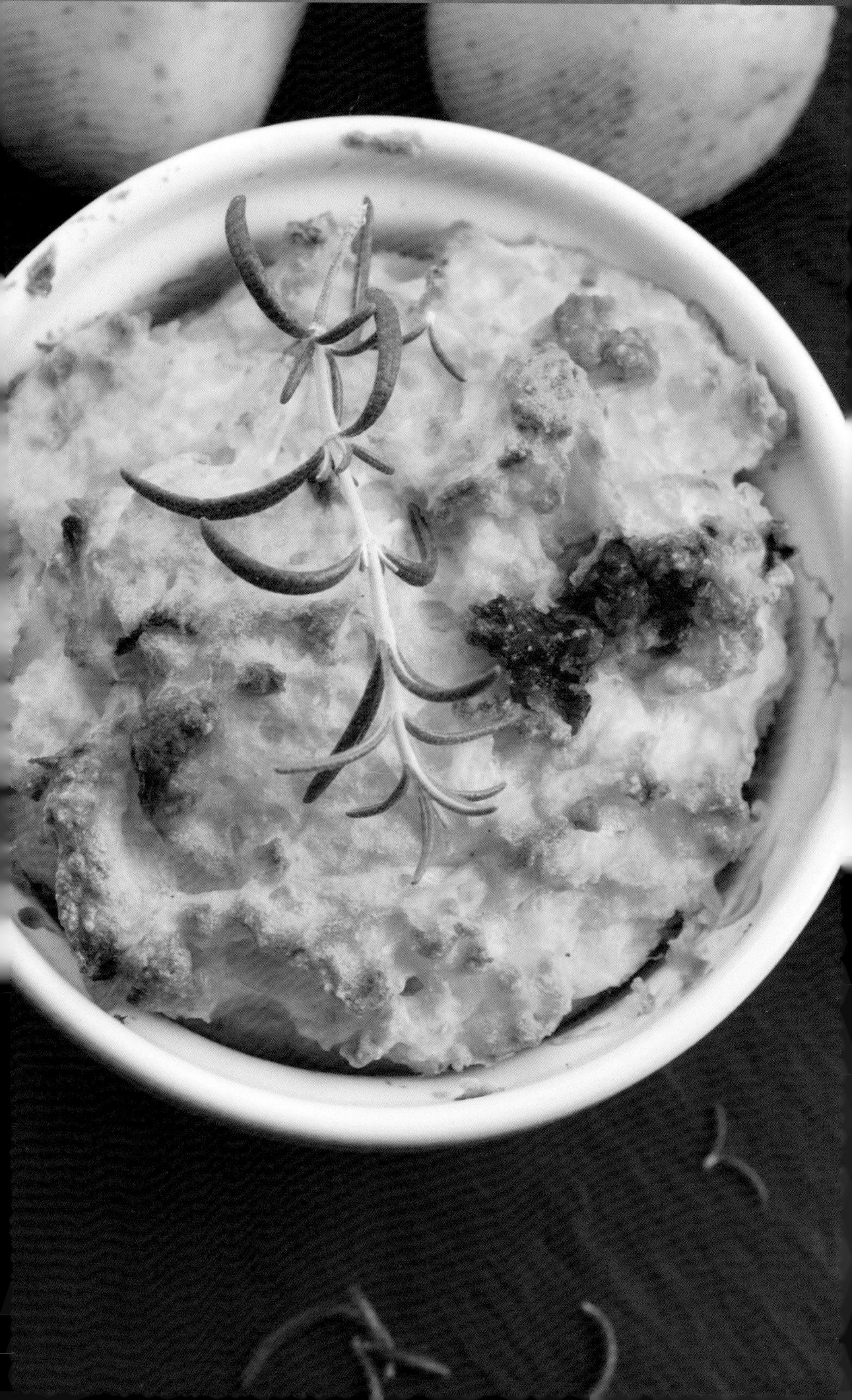

Drop Cookies

You would never guess these comforting, soft cookies have potatoes in the mix.

Butter (or hard margarine), softened	1/2 cup	125 mL
Brown sugar, packed	1 cup	250 mL
Large egg, fork-beaten	1	1
Orange flavoring	1/2 tsp.	2 mL
Lemon flavoring	1/2 tsp.	2 mL
Mashed potatoes	1 cup	250 mL
Chopped walnuts	1/2 cup	125 mL
All-purpose flour	1 1/2 cups	375 mL
Baking powder	1 tsp.	5 mL
Baking soda	1/2 tsp.	2 mL
Salt	1/4 tsp.	1 mL
Maraschino cherries, drained and blotted dry, halved	21	21

Cream butter and sugar together in a medium bowl. Beat in egg.

Add both flavourings and potato and mix well. Stir in walnuts.

Stir flour, baking powder, baking soda and salt in a small bowl. Add to batter and stir to moisten. Drop by tablespoonfuls (15 mL) onto a greased baking sheet. Dent top of each cookie with your thumb of back of a spoon. Bake in 350°F (175°C) oven for 5 minutes. Remove from oven and press dents again. Bake for 10 to 15 minutes. Let stand on baking sheet for 5 minutes before removing to a wire rack to cool. Place 1 cherry half in each dent. Makes 42 cookies.

1 cookie: 80 Calories; 3.5 g Total Fat (0.5 g Mono, 1 g Poly, 1.5 g Sat); 10 mg Cholesterol; 11 g Carbohydrate (0 g Fibre, 6 g Sugar); 1 g Protein; 55 mg Sodium

Chocolate Cookies

A cakey-type soft cookie with rich chocolate flavor.

Butter (or hard margarine), softened	1/2 cup	125 mL
Granulated sugar	1/2 cup	125 mL
Brown sugar, packed	1/2 cup	125 mL
Large egg	1	1
Mashed potatoes	1/2 cup	125 mL
Vanilla extract	1/2 tsp.	2 mL
Buttermilk (or soured milk, see Tip, below)	3/4 cup	175 mL
All-purpose flour	2 cups	500 mL
Cocoa	1/3 cup	75 mL
Baking soda	1/2 tsp.	2 mL
Salt	1/2 tsp.	2 mL

Cream butter and both sugars together in a large bowl.

Mix in egg, potato, vanilla and buttermilk.

Add remaining 4 ingredients and stir to moisten. Drop dough by rounded tablespoonfuls (15 mL) onto a greased baking sheet. Bake in 400°F (200°C) oven for 10 minutes. Makes 4 dozen cookies.

1 cookie: 60 Calories; 2 g Total Fat (0.5 g Mono, 0 g Poly, 1.5 g Sat); 10 mg Cholesterol; 9 g Carbohydrate (0 g Fibre, 4 g Sugar); 1 g Protein; 45 mg Sodium

Tip: To make soured milk, measure 1 tbsp. (15 mL) white vinegar or lemon juice into a 1 cup (250 mL) liquid measure. Add enough milk to make 1 cup (250 mL), and stir gently. Let stand for 1 minute.

Candy Squares

Coconut macaroon base with a thick chocolate top. Reminds you of a certain chocolate bar!

Mashed potatoes	1/2 cup	125 mL
Butter (or hard margarine), softened	1 tbsp.	15 mL
Vanilla extract	1 tsp.	5 mL
Salt	1/4 tsp.	1 mL
Icing (confectioner's) sugar	3 cups	750 mL
Medium unsweetened coconut	2 1/2 cups	625 mL
Semisweet chocolate chips	1 1/2 cup	375 mL
Butter (or hard margarine)	3 tbsp.	45 mL

Combine potato, first amount of butter, vanilla and salt in a large bowl.

Mix in icing sugar and coconut. Shape mixture into mounds using a tablespoon.

Melt chocolate chips and second amount of butter in a medium saucepan on low, stirring often. Dip each piece in chocolate and set on a rack placed on a baking tray lined with parchment paper. Chill for 1 hour. Makes 50 pieces.

1 piece: 80 Calories; 4 g Total Fat (0 g Mono, 0 g Poly, 3 g Sat); 0 mg Cholesterol; 12 g Carbohydrate (1 g Fibre, 10 g Sugar); 0 g Protein; 20 mg Sodium

Sweet Potato Brownies

The flavours of sweet potato casserole in rich, chocolatey brownie form! If you don't have any cooked sweet potato on hand, you can use canned.

Granulated sugar	1 cup	250 mL
All-purpose flour	3/4 cup	175 mL
Cocoa, sifted if lumpy	1/2 cup	125 mL
Whole-wheat flour	1/2 cup	125 mL
Baking powder	1 tsp.	5 mL
Salt	1/4 tsp.	1 mL
Semi-sweet chocolate baking squares (1 oz., 28 g, each), chopped	2	2
Large eggs	2	2
Mashed orange-fleshed sweet potato (about 3/4 lb., 340 g, uncooked)	1 cup	250 mL
Buttermilk (or soured milk, see Tip, page 146)	1/2 cup	125 mL
Cooking oil	1/4 cup	60 mL
Vanilla extract	1 tsp.	5 mL
Ground cinnamon	1/2 tsp.	2 mL
Miniature marshmallows	2 cups	500 mL
Semi-sweet chocolate chips	1/3 cup	75 mL

Combine first 6 ingredients in a medium bowl. Make a well in centre.

Microwave chocolate in a small microwave-safe bowl on Medium for about 90 seconds, stirring every 30 seconds until almost melted (see Tip, page 12). Stir until smooth.

Put next 6 ingredients into a blender or food processor. Add chocolate and process until smooth. Add to well. Stir until just combined. Spread in greased 9 x 9 inch (23 x 23 cm) pan. Bake in 350°F (175°C) oven for about 35 minutes until wooden pick inserted in centre comes out moist but not wet with batter. Do not overbake.

Scatter marshmallows and chocolate chips over top. Broil on centre rack in oven for 1 to 2 minutes until golden. Let stand in pan on a wire rack until cool. Cuts into 36 pieces.

1 piece: 85 Calories; 3 g Total Fat (1 g Mono, 0 g Poly, 1 g Sat); 0 mg Cholesterol; 15 g Carbohydrate (1 g Fibre, 9 g Sugar); 1 g Protein; 35 mg Sodium

Sweet Potato Pie

Looks just like pumpkin pie—and almost tastes like it too! Serve with a dollop of whipped cream.

Fresh sweet potatoes (with peel), blemishes removed	1 1/2 lbs.	680 g
Cans of evaporated milk (not skim), 5 1/2 oz. (160 mL) each	2	2
Granulated sugar	1/2 cup	125 mL
Brown sugar, packed	1/3 cup	75 mL
All-purpose flour	1 1/2 tbsp.	22 mL
Ground cinnamon	1/2 tsp.	2 mL
Ground nutmeg	1/4 tsp.	1 mL
Large eggs	2	2
Vanilla extract	1/4 tsp.	1 mL
Pastry for 9 inch (23 cm) deep dish pie shell	1	1

Cook sweet potato in boiling salted water in a large pot or Dutch oven on medium-high until soft but not mushy. Drain. Run under cold water to cool and drain well. Peel and discard skin. Chop coarsely.

Process sweet potato and evaporated milk in a blender or food processor until smooth.

Combine next 5 ingredients in a large bowl.

Add eggs, vanilla and sweet potato mixture. Beat until smooth.

Roll out pastry on a lightly floured surface to about 1/8 inch (3 mm) thickness. Line pie plate. Trim, leaving 1/2 inch (12 mm) overhang. Roll under and crimp decorative edge. Pour filling into pie shell. Bake on bottom rack in 425°F (220°C) oven for 15 minutes. Reduce heat to 350°F (175°C). Bake for about 45 minutes until knife inserted in centre comes out clean. Pie might puff up but will settle when cooling. Let stand on wire rack for at least 30 minutes before serving. Cuts into 8 wedges.

1 wedge: 320 Calories; 10 g Total Fat (4 g Mono, 1 g Poly, 4 g Sat); 65 mg Cholesterol; 52 g Carbohydrate (3 g Fibre, 26 g Sugar); 7 g Protein; 220 mg Sodium

Chocolate Cake

Mashed potatoes make this unique cake moist and tender. The icing also includes mashed potatoes, eliminating the need for dairy products or fat.

Butter (or hard margarine), softened	1/2 cup	125 mL
Granulated sugar	1 cup	250 mL
Large eggs	2	2
Vanilla extract	1 tsp.	5 mL
Buttermilk (or soured milk, see Tip, 146)	1 cup	250 mL
Mashed potatoes	1 cup	250 mL
All-purpose flour	1 3/4 cups	425 mL
Cocoa, sifted	1/3 cup	75 mL
Baking powder	1 tsp.	5 mL
Baking soda	1/2 tsp.	2 mL
Ground cinnamon	1/2 tsp.	2 mL
Salt	1/2 tsp.	2 mL
Warm mashed potatoes	1/4 cup	60 mL
Icing (confectioner's) sugar	2 3/4 cups	675 mL
Cocoa, sifted	2 tbsp.	30 mL
Vanilla extract	1/2 tsp.	2 mL
Warm water (or coffee), approximately	2 tbsp.	30 mL

Cream butter and sugar in a large bowl. Beat in eggs, 1 at a time. Stir in vanilla.

Slowly beat buttermilk into potato in a small bowl until smooth. Beat into egg mixture.

Stir next 6 ingredients in a medium bowl. Add to potato mixture. Beat slowly to incorporate flour. Beat on medium for about 1 minute until smooth. Turn into a greased 9 x 9 inch (23 x 23 cm) pan. Bake, uncovered, in 350°F (175°C) oven for about 40 minutes until wooden pick inserted in centre comes out clean. Set aside to cool.

For the icing, sieve or rice second amount of potatoes into a medium bowl.

Sift icing sugar and cocoa into potatoes and stir well.

Slowly beat in second amount of vanilla and water, adding more water or icing sugar to make desired spreading consistency. Spread over top and sides of cooled cake. Cuts into 16 pieces.

1 piece: 250 Calories; 7 g Total Fat (2 g Mono, 0 g Poly, 4 g Sat); 45 mg Cholesterol; 45 g Carbohydrate (30 g Fibre, 1 g Sugar); 3 g Protein; 190 mg Sodium

Sweet Potato Cheesecake

Sweet potato might seem like an odd addition to a cheesecake, but the end result is delicious and lighter than most cheesecakes. You can use canned sweet potatoes if you do not have any fresh ones on hand.

Butter (or hard margarine)	1/4 cup	60 mL
Gingersnap cookie crumbs	1 1/4 cups	300 mL
Light cream cheese, softened	8 oz.	250 g
Granulated sugar	1/2 cup	125 mL
Light creamed cottage cheese,	1 cup	250 mL
Mashed sweet potatoes	2 1/4 cups	550 mL
All-purpose flour	2 tbsp.	30 mL
Ground cinnamon	3/4 tsp.	4 mL
Ground nutmeg	1/2 tsp.	2 mL
Ground ginger	1/2 tsp.	2 mL
Large eggs	2	2

For the crust, melt butter in a medium saucepan and stir in gingersnap crumbs. Press mixture firmly on bottom of an ungreased 9 inch (23 cm) springform pan. Bake in 350°F (175°C) oven for 10 minutes.

For the filling, beat cream cheese, sugar and cottage cheese until smooth. Mix in sweet potato, flour, cinnamon, nutmeg and ginger.

Add eggs, 1 at a time, beating on low just to mix in. Turn into crust. Bake in 350°F (175°C) oven for about 60 minutes until firm. Run a knife around top edge of cheesecake so it will settle evenly. Cool, then chill. Cuts into 12 wedges.

1 wedge: 220 Calories; 10 g Total Fat (2 g Mono, 0 g Poly, 6 g Sat); 60 mg Cholesterol; 25 g Carbohydrate (1 g Fibre, 14 g Sugar); 6 g Protein; 300 mg Sodium

Index